LIAM BENEDICT

VÍA DE LA PLATA CAMINO TRAVEL GUIDE

YOUR COMPREHENSIVE GUIDE TO WALKING SPAIN'S ANCIENT ROUTE: HISTORY, STAGES, IMAGES, AND ACCOMMODATION TIPS FOR PILGRIMS

Copyright © 2025 by LIAM BENEDICT

All rights reserved. No part of this publication may be reproduced, stored or transmitted in any form or by any means, electronic, mechanical, photocopying, recording, scanning, or otherwise without written permission from the publisher. It is illegal to copy this book, post it to a website, or distribute it by any other means without permission.

LIAM BENEDICT asserts the moral right to be identified as the author of this work.

First edition

This book was professionally typeset on Reedsy.
Find out more at reedsy.com

*For the intrepid souls who seek both adventure and meaning,
this guide is dedicated to you.*

*May your footsteps along the VÍA DE LA PLATA path
bring discovery, peace, and a deeper connection
to the history and spirit of this ancient route.*

*Walk with open hearts and curious minds,
may this guide light your way and enrich every step.*

Contents

Disclaimer	vi
SCAN THE QR CODE	vii
Introduction	1
Welcome to the Via de la Plata	1
About the Route: History and Significance	1
Via de la Plata vs. Camino Francés: What Makes This Route Special	2

I   Planning Your Journey

1 Chapter One	7
Before You Go	7
Best Time to Walk the Via de la Plata	7
How Long Does It Take?	9
Physical Preparation and Training	11
Choosing Your Starting Point: Seville, Mérida, or Beyond	17
Budget Planning and Costs	19
Travel Insurance Considerations	20
2 Chapter Two	21
What to Bring	21
Essential Gear Checklist	21
Clothing for Variable Weather	22
Footwear: Choosing the Right Boots or Shoes	24
Backpack Selection and Packing Tips	26
First Aid and Medical Supplies	28
What to Leave at Home	30

3	Chapter Three	31
	Logistics and Practicalities	31
	Getting to Seville (or Your Starting Point)	31
	Getting Home from Santiago de Compostela	33
	Credential and Compostela: What You Need to Know	35
	Accommodation Options: Albergues, Hotels, and Hostels	38
	Booking Strategy: When to Reserve Ahead	40
	Food and Water Along the Route	41
	Language Basics: Essential Spanish Phrases	42
	Money Matters: ATMs, Cards, and Cash	45
4	Chapter Four	48
	Health and Safety	48
	Common Injuries and How to Prevent Them	48
	Dealing with Blisters	49
	Heat and Sun Protection	50
	Wildlife and Natural Hazards	52
	Walking Alone vs. in Groups	52
	Safety Tips for Solo Travelers	55
II	The Route – Stage by Stage	
5	Chapter Five	59
	Andalusia – Seville to Extremadura (Stages 1–9)	59
	Stage 1: Seville to Guillena	59
	Stage 2: Guillena to Castilblanco de los Arroyos (22km)	62
	Stage 3: Castilblanco to Almadén de la Plata (29 km)	63
	Stage 4: Almadén de la Plata to Monesterio	64
	Stage 5: Monesterio to Fuente de Cantos (21km)	67
	Stage 6: Fuente de Cantos to Zafra	68
	Stage 7: Zafra to Villafranca de los Barros (20 km)	69
	Stage 8: Villafranca to Torremejía	69
	Stage 9: Torremejía to Mérida	72
6	Chapter Six	74

Extremadura - Heart of the Via (Stages 10-20) 74
   Stage 10: Mérida to Aljucén 74
   Stage 11: Aljucén to Alcuéscar 75
   Stage 12: Alcuéscar to Cáceres 75
   Stage 13: Cáceres to Embalse de Alcántara 77
   Stage 14: Embalse de Alcántara to Grimaldo 78
   Stage 15: Grimaldo to Carcaboso 79
   Stage 16: Carcaboso to Aldeanueva del Camino 80
   Stage 17: Aldeanueva to La Calzada de Béjar (22 km) 81
   Stage 18: La Calzada to Fuenterroble de Salvatierra 82
   Stage 19: Fuenterroble to San Pedro de Rozados 83
   Stage 20: San Pedro to Salamanca 84

7 Chapter Seven 86
ountains and Meseta (Stages 21-28) 86
   Stage 21: Salamanca to El Cubo de la Tierra del Vino 86
   Stage 22: El Cubo to Zamora 87
   Stage 23: Zamora to Montamarta 88
   Stage 24: Montamarta to Granja de Moreruela 89
   Stage 25: Granja de Moreruela to Tábara 89
   Stage 26: Tábara to Santa Croya de Tera 91
   Stage 27: Santa Croya to Rionegro del Puente 91
   Stage 28: Rionegro to Puebla de Sanabria 93

8 Chapter Eight 95
Galicia and Final Approach 95
   Stage 29: Puebla de Sanabria to Lubián 95
   Stage 30: Lubián to A Gudiña 96
   Stage 31: A Gudiña to Laza 98
   Stage 32: Laza to Xunqueira de Ambía 99
   Stage 33: Xunqueira to Ourense 99
   Alternative Routes: Via Sanabrés vs. joining the Camino Francés at Astorga 101
   Ourense to Santiago via Sanabrés Route (overview of remaining stages) 102

9	Chapter Nine	104
	Arrival in Santiago de Compostela	104
	The Final Approach to Santiago	104
	Cathedral and Pilgrim Mass	105
	Obtaining Your Compostela	106
	What to Do in Santiago: Top Sites and Experiences	107
	Rest and Recovery	108
	Pilgrim Farewell Rituals	109
III	Cultural and Historical Context	
10	Chapter Ten	113
	History of the Via de la Plata	113
	Pre-Roman Origins	113
	The Roman Road: Iter ab Emerita Asturicam	114
	Medieval Pilgrimage Development	115
	Modern Revival and Recognition	117
	Archaeological Sites Along the Route	118
11	Chapter Eleven	120
	Art and Architecture	120
	Roman Engineering: Bridges, Milestones, and Roads	120
	Romanesque Churches of Zamora	121
	Gothic Cathedrals: Salamanca and Beyond	122
12	Chapter Twelve	124
	Local Culture and Traditions	124
	Festivals and Celebrations Along the Route	124
	Traditional Cuisine by Region	125
	Wine Regions: Ribera del Guadiana to Ribeiro	127
	Local Crafts and Products	128
13	Chapter Thirteen	130
	Food and Drink Guide	130
	Andalusian Tapas and Gazpacho	130
	Extremaduran Specialties: Jamón Ibérico and Torta del Casar	131

Castilian Roasts and Hearty Stews	132
Galician Seafood and Pulpo	132
Regional Wines and Beverages	133
Vegetarian and Special Dietary Options	134

IV Resources

14 Chapter Fourteen	139
Practical Directory	139
Tourist Offices and Information Centers	139
Medical Facilities Along the Route	140
Gear Shops and Services	142
Transport Connections	143
Luggage Transfer Services	143
Useful Apps	144
15 Chapter Fifteen	146
Spanish Language Guide	146
Essential Phrases for Pilgrims	146
Menu Vocabulary	148
Medical and Emergency Terms	150
Numbers, Days, and Directions	151
Cultural Etiquette	152
Nightlife and Entertainment	153
BUDGET PLANNER	155
TRAVEL JOURNAL	158

Disclaimer

Thank you for choosing this guide as your companion on the VÍA DE LA PLATA journey! While every effort has been made to provide accurate and helpful information, please remember that travel experiences can vary. Conditions on the route, accommodations, and other details may change, so it's always good to double-check and be prepared for surprises along the way.

This guide is here to inspire and assist you, but your safety and enjoyment depend on your own decisions and judgments. Walk with an open heart, stay curious, and embrace the adventure—this book is your friendly guide, not a rulebook. Enjoy every step!

SCAN THE QR CODE

How to Scan a QR Code

- Open your phone's camera or QR-scanner app.

- Hold your device steady and point it at the QR code.
- Make sure the entire code is visible in the frame.
- Wait a moment for the scanner to recognize it.
- It'll take you directly to the PDF image

Thanks for reading:)

Introduction

Welcome to the Via de la Plata

Welcome to the Vía de la Plata , an ancient route steeped in history, culture, and breathtaking landscapes. As you embark on this unique pilgrimage or adventure, you join countless travelers who have walked this path for centuries, discovering not just the beauty of Spain's diverse regions, but also a journey of personal growth and reflection.

Whether you are walking for spiritual reasons, the love of nature, or the thrill of exploration, the Vía de la Plata offers a rich tapestry of experiences. From vibrant cities to tranquil villages, Roman ruins to medieval architecture, and rolling countryside to majestic mountains, this route invites you to connect deeply with the past and present of this incredible land.

This guide is designed to be your trusted companion every step of the way—helping you plan, prepare, and fully enjoy the adventure that awaits on the Vía de la Plata . Welcome, and buen camino!

About the Route: History and Significance

The Vía de la Plata is an ancient and historically significant route that traces back to pre-Roman times. Originally used as a natural passageway linking the Iberian plateau with the southern region of Andalusia, it evolved into a key Roman road connecting important settlements such as Augusta Emerita (modern Mérida) and Asturica Augusta (modern Astorga). This engineering marvel facilitated trade, military movements, and cultural exchange across western Spain.

The name Vía de la Plata, often translated as the "Silver Way," is believed to stem from a linguistic evolution rather than a direct reference to silver itself. One theory suggests it originated from the Arabic term *bal'latta*, meaning "paved road," reflecting the Moorish influence during their rule of the Iberian Peninsula. The route gained renewed prominence during the Middle Ages as a pilgrimage path to Santiago de Compostela, serving pilgrims traveling from the south of Spain.

Throughout history, the Vía de la Plata has borne witness to significant events including Roman colonization, Moorish incursions, and Christian reconquest. It became not only a military and trade artery but also a spiritual journey for thousands of pilgrims. Today, the route remains a living heritage road, blending ancient infrastructure with medieval chapels and vibrant local cultures, inviting pilgrims and travelers to experience its historical depth and natural beauty.

Via de la Plata vs. Camino Francés: What Makes This Route Special

The Vía de la Plata and the Camino Francés are two of the most iconic pilgrimage routes to Santiago de Compostela, each offering unique experiences and charms. What sets the Vía de la Plata apart is its blend of historical depth, diverse landscapes, and a quieter, less crowded journey. While the Camino Francés is famed for its bustling pilgrim traffic, well-established infrastructure, and classic northern scenery, the Vía de la Plata winds through the heart of Spain's varied regions—from the warm Andalusian plains to the rugged mountains of Castilla y León and the lush greenery of Galicia.

The Vía de la Plata holds a distinct Mediterranean ambiance with rich Roman and Moorish heritage visible along the route, giving walkers a deep cultural and archaeological experience. Its quieter pathways allow for more introspective travel and closer interactions with local communities who retain strong traditional customs and cuisine. Additionally, the Vía de la Plata is generally longer and more physically challenging than the Camino Francés, making it appealing to those seeking a more solitary and adventurous

INTRODUCTION

pilgrimage.

In summary, the Vía de la Plata offers pilgrims a special combination of historical resonance, cultural richness, and intimate connection with Spain's diverse landscapes and people, all away from the crowds typically found on the Camino Francés.

I

Planning Your Journey

1

Chapter One

Before You Go

Best Time to Walk the Via de la Plata

The ideal time to walk the Vía de la Plata depends on your preferences for weather, crowds, and physical challenges. Each season offers distinct advantages and challenges.

Spring (March-May)

- Spring is arguably the best time overall. Temperatures range from 15-25°C (59-77°F), creating comfortable walking conditions without extreme heat. Wildflowers bloom across Extremadura and Galicia, painting the landscape in vibrant colors. Water sources are abundant from winter rainfall, and albergues are moderately busy without peak-season overcrowding. The downside is occasional rain and mud, particularly in Galicia. Many pilgrims choose April-May when conditions stabilize and flowers peak.

Summer (June-August)

- Summer brings challenges and rewards. Andalusian and Extremaduran stages can reach 35-40°C (95-104°F), demanding early morning starts and afternoon siesta breaks. Water becomes precious in some sections, requiring careful planning. Crowds increase significantly, especially July-August, filling albergues and creating social energy. Advantages include long daylight hours, reliable weather, and vibrant festival seasons. Summer suits experienced walkers comfortable with heat and social pilgrimage.

Autumn (September-November)

- Autumn rivals spring for optimal conditions. Temperatures cool to 15-22°C (59-72°F) as summer heat fades. Golden light and harvest seasons create stunning photography opportunities. Fewer pilgrims mean quieter trails and easier albergue availability. September remains warm, while October-November introduce misty mornings and occasional rain. Autumn is perfect for solitude seekers and photographers.

Winter (December-February)

- Winter presents the harshest conditions but rewards committed pilgrims with profound solitude. Northern stages, particularly Galicia, experience rain, mud, and occasional snow at higher elevations. Temperatures drop to 5-10°C (41-50°F), requiring proper gear. Many albergues close seasonally. Services become sparse. However, winter pilgrims experience unmatched intimacy with the landscape and spiritual deepening. Only recommended for experienced walkers with winter hiking experience.

Practical Recommendations

For first-time pilgrims, **April-May or September-October** offer the best balance of comfortable weather, manageable crowds, and reliable services. These windows provide ideal conditions across all regions without extreme challenges.

For solitude seekers, **November** offers quietness without severe winter conditions, or **early March** catches spring's beginning before crowds.

For experienced walkers seeking challenge and spiritual depth, **winter or summer extremes** provide transformative experiences—just prepare accordingly with proper gear and realistic expectations.

Consider also that Xacobeo (Holy Years, when July 25 falls on Sunday) bring increased pilgrims and festival energy to Santiago, making spring and autumn preferable for avoiding these years if solitude matters.

Ultimately, the best time is when you can commit fully to the journey. Each season transforms the pilgrimage into a distinct experience—choose based on your fitness level, preferences, and available time.

How Long Does It Take?

Walking the full Vía de la Plata from Seville to Santiago covers 1,000 km (621 miles) in 40-50 days at 20-25 km daily stages, including 3-5 rest days for recovery amid 17,500m total elevation and long isolated sections demanding consistent pacing. Fit pilgrims average 5-6 hours moving time per stage (4-5 km/h), but beginners extend to 7-8 hours factoring fatigue, weather, and sightseeing in cities like Salamanca or Mérida. Shorter sections suit time constraints: Seville-Mérida (214 km) takes 8-10 days; full Mérida-Santiago needs 30-40 days; the final Ourense-Santiago (100 km) requires just 5-7 days to qualify for Compostela.

Stage Breakdowns by Section: Divide the route into logical segments for planning, with typical stage lengths and days based on official guides and pilgrim reports.

1. Section: Seville to Mérida

- Distance: 214 km
- Stages: 9-10
- Days: 8-10

- Key Challenges: Heat, asphalt (50 km+), early isolation

2. Section: Mérida to Salamanca

    - Distance: 300 km
    - Stages: 12-14
    - Days: 12-15
    - Key Challenges: Dehesa plains, 30 km gaps without services

3. Section: Salamanca to Zamora/Astorga

    - Distance: 200 km
    - Stages: 8-9
    - Days: 8-10
    - Key Challenges: Rolling hills, Roman bridges

4. Section: Zamora to Ourense (Sanabrés)

    - Distance: 200 km
    - Stages: 9-10
    - Days: 9-11
    - Key Challenges: Climbs like Pico Tres Mogotes

5. Section: Ourense to Santiago

    - Distance: 100 km
    - Stages: 4-5
    - Days: 5-7
    - Key Challenges: Lush Galicia, final ascents

Total stages: 36-38 depending on splits; cyclists halve to 16.

Factors Affecting Duration

Pace varies by fitness (sedentary: +10-20% time), pack weight (6-10 kg slows 10%), and season—summer heat adds breaks, winter mud extends. Luggage transfer services enable 25-30 km days; back-to-back longs (e.g., 33 km Casar de Cáceres-Cañaveral) test limits, so build buffers for 1-2 zero days weekly.

Physical Preparation and Training

Walking 1,000+ kilometers over 40-50 days demands serious physical preparation. Proper training prevents injuries, builds endurance, and ensures you complete the pilgrimage enjoying rather than enduring it.

Pre-Pilgrimage Training Timeline
   Three Months Before:

- Begin with a foundation of cardiovascular fitness. Walk 30-45 minutes daily at a comfortable pace, gradually increasing to 60 minutes. Mix flat terrain with gentle hills. Incorporate strength training 2-3 times weekly, focusing on legs, core, and glutes—these muscles bear pilgrimage stress. Start carrying a weighted backpack (10-15 pounds) on long walks to simulate actual conditions.

Two Months Before:

- Increase walking distance to 10-15 km (6-9 miles) on weekends. Include hill training—stairs, inclines, or mountains strengthen legs for Galician terrain. Add cross-training: swimming, cycling, or elliptical work develops cardiovascular endurance without constant impact. Continue strength training with emphasis on single-leg exercises (lunges, step-ups) to build stability. Carry your actual pilgrim backpack (packed to actual weight) on longer walks.

One Month Before:

- Perform 15-20 km practice walks in terrain similar to your route. If possible, walk consecutive days to condition your feet and body to sustained effort. Practice with full gear—boots broken in, backpack adjusted properly, hydration system functional. Do a "test hike" of 25+ km to experience how your body responds to extended walking. Identify and address any discomfort before departure.

Two Weeks Before:

- Reduce intensity slightly—maintain fitness without exhausting yourself. Focus on flexibility and injury prevention through stretching and foam rolling. Practice foot care: trim toenails, address any existing blisters or calluses with medical attention. Break in boots completely; no new footwear on pilgrimage day.

Recommended Training Schedule
Week 1-4 (Base Building):

- Monday: Rest or gentle yoga (30 min)
- Tuesday: Strength training (45 min)
- Wednesday: Walk 5-8 km at moderate pace
- Thursday: Strength training (45 min)
- Friday: Rest or cross-training
- Saturday: Long walk 8-12 km
- Sunday: Rest or gentle activity

Week 5-8 (Building Endurance):

- Monday: Rest or yoga (30-45 min)
- Tuesday: Strength training (45-60 min) with heavy focus
- Wednesday: Walk 10-12 km with backpack
- Thursday: Strength training (45 min)
- Friday: Cross-training (30-45 min)

- Saturday: Long walk 12-18 km with full pack
- Sunday: Rest or 5 km easy walk

Week 9-12 (Peak Training):

- Monday: Rest or recovery yoga (45 min)
- Tuesday: Strength training (45 min, maintenance)
- Wednesday: Walk 12-15 km with backpack, varied terrain
- Thursday: Rest or cross-training (30 min)
- Friday: Walk 8-10 km easy pace
- Saturday: Long walk 15-25 km, simulating consecutive days if possible
- Sunday: Complete rest

Week 13-14 (Taper):

- Reduce intensity by 20-30%
- Maintain walking fitness without exhaustion
- Focus on recovery and flexibility
- Final gear testing and adjustments

Strength Training Focus

Pilgrimage places specific demands on your body. Target these areas:

- **Legs and Glutes:** Squats, lunges, step-ups, calf raises, single-leg deadlifts. Strong legs prevent knee and hip pain—common pilgrimage injuries. Perform 2-3 sets of 10-15 reps, 2-3 times weekly.
- **Core Stability:** Planks, side planks, dead bugs, bird dogs, bridges. A strong core maintains posture during long walking hours, preventing lower back strain. Hold planks 30-60 seconds, 3-4 sets.
- **Hip Stability:** Clamshells, side-lying leg raises, monster walks with resistance bands. Hip stability prevents knee tracking issues and IT band problems.
- **Foot and Ankle Strength:** Toe raises, single-leg stands, balance board

work. Strong feet and ankles reduce blister risk and improve stability on rocky terrain.
- **Back Strength:** Rows, reverse flyes, superman holds. Backpack carrying demands strong backs. Prevent shoulder and neck tension.

Cardiovascular Conditioning

Build aerobic capacity supporting sustained walking:

- **Walking:** The best training is walking itself. Accumulate 100+ miles on feet before pilgrimage.
- **Hiking:** Include elevation gain—stairs, hills, mountains. Galician terrain demands hill fitness.
- **Cycling:** Low-impact endurance building, 30-60 minutes, 2-3 times weekly.
- **Swimming:** Full-body conditioning without impact stress, excellent for recovery days.
- **Elliptical:** Controlled impact, maintains fitness on bad-weather training days.

Aim for 150 minutes of moderate-intensity cardio or 75 minutes of vigorous cardio weekly during preparation months.

Flexibility and Injury Prevention

Tight muscles cause pilgrimage suffering. Daily stretching prevents injuries:

- **Dynamic stretches before walking:** Leg swings, arm circles, walking lunges (5-10 minutes)
- **Static stretches after walking:** Hold 30 seconds each leg—hamstrings, quads, calves, hip flexors, glutes (15-20 minutes)
- **Foam rolling:** 1-2 minutes per major muscle group 3-4 times weekly reduces muscle tension
- **Yoga:** 2-3 times weekly improves flexibility, balance, and mental clarity.

Restorative yoga aids recovery.

Focus on tight areas common in pilgrims: calves, hamstrings, IT band, hip flexors, lower back.

Nutrition and Hydration Training
Train your digestive system for pilgrimage demands:

- **Practice eating while walking:** Consume energy bars, nuts, fruit while moving to avoid stomach upset
- **Hydration strategy:** Drink 500 ml (17 oz) water every 30 minutes during training walks; establish rhythm
- **Electrolyte practice:** Try sports drinks, electrolyte tablets, or natural options (coconut water) during long walks
- **Breakfast routine:** Eat breakfast 1-2 hours before walking; avoid starting fasting
- **Post-walk recovery:** Consume protein and carbs within 30 minutes of finishing long walks

Mental Training
Physical preparation matters, but mental resilience determines pilgrimage completion:

- **Visualize success:** Imagine walking challenging terrain confidently, overcoming difficulties, arriving in Santiago
- **Set realistic goals:** Don't aim for daily speed records; focus on consistent, sustainable pacing
- **Practice solitude:** Take training walks alone to build confidence in solo pilgrimage
- **Develop mantras:** Create motivational phrases for difficult moments ("One step at a time," "I am strong")
- **Journal training experiences:** Record how your body responds, emotional shifts, growing confidence

Pre-Pilgrimage Medical Checkup

Before committing 40-50 days to pilgrimage, consult your doctor:

- Full physical exam including cardiovascular assessment
- Discuss any joint or muscle concerns
- Address any medical conditions potentially affected by sustained walking
- Review medications and pilgrimage compatibility
- Get professional foot assessment—podiatrist evaluation prevents blister disasters
- Ensure vaccinations current (especially if traveling internationally)
- Consider travel insurance covering pilgrimage-related incidents

Common Training Mistakes to Avoid

- **Ramping up too fast:** Increase mileage gradually (10% weekly maximum)
- **Ignoring pain:** Address minor discomfort immediately before it becomes injury
- **Skipping strength training:** Relying solely on walking builds endurance but weak muscles cause injuries
- **Poor footwear choices:** Train in pilgrimage boots, not casual shoes
- **Inadequate recovery:** Rest days are training, not laziness; muscles rebuild during recovery
- **No backpack training:** Carrying weight changes mechanics; train with actual load
- **Neglecting flexibility:** Tight muscles limit range of motion, causing compensatory injuries

Fitness Assessment Before Pilgrimage

Two weeks before departure, honestly assess readiness:

- Can you walk 20 km comfortably in a day with a loaded backpack? Can you do 30 km with extra effort but without pain? Can you walk three consecutive days without severe fatigue? If yes to all, you're ready. If no, consider postponing and extending training, or choosing a shorter partial route.

Timeline Summary

- **Sedentary to Pilgrimage Ready:** 12-14 weeks minimum
- **Already active to Pilgrimage Ready:** 8-10 weeks
- **Experienced hiker to Pilgrimage Ready:** 4-6 weeks maintenance
- **Injured or recovering:** 16+ weeks tailored training

Proper physical preparation transforms pilgrimage from suffering into joy. The investment in training pays dividends in pain-free walking, faster recovery, injury prevention, and overall enjoyment. Your body will thank you for months afterward, and you'll finish stronger than you started.

Choosing Your Starting Point: Seville, Mérida, or Beyond

Where you begin your journey on the Vía de la Plata shapes your pilgrimage's length, terrain, history, and spiritual experience.

Seville: The Classic Starting Point

- Seville is the traditional and most popular starting point for the full Vía de la Plata. The route from Sevilla covers approximately 1,000 km to Santiago. Beginning here means you experience the complete transformation from the warm, Moorish landscapes of Andalusia, through Extremadura's rolling plains, Castilla y León's plateau, and into lush green Galicia. Seville is well-connected by train and air, and starting here maximizes the historical and physical challenge—this is the "full journey" recognized by most pilgrims.

Mérida: A Balanced Choice

- Mérida lies about 200 km north of Seville and is a common starting point for those who want a shorter pilgrimage but still crave authentic Roman and medieval waypoints. Starting in Mérida means your route spans about 800 km. Mérida's incredible Roman ruins—amphitheater, aqueduct, and temples—make it historically significant, and the terrain from here is varied, combining Extremadura's nature with the later Castilian and Galician stages. Trains connect Mérida with major Spanish cities.

Zamora, Salamanca, or Beyond: Shorter Options

- Starting in Zamora or Salamanca gives you a journey of 350–400 km, ideal for those with limited time or seeking the Compostela with a quieter, northern route. These cities offer cultural richness and avoid the hottest southern stretches. Many choose Ourense (about 100–120 km from Santiago) as a week-long pilgrimage to receive the official Compostela certificate.

Tips for Choosing

- For the classic long-distance challenge and historical experience, start in Sevilla.
- If you desire variety but have five to six weeks, Mérida is a strong choice.
- For a two- or three-week journey, begin in Zamora, Salamanca, or Ourense.
- Factor in seasonal weather, transport links, and your physical preparation.

No matter where you begin, each starting point on the Vía de la Plata offers a richly rewarding and transformative pilgrimage.

CHAPTER ONE

Budget Planning and Costs

Walking the Vía de la Plata typically costs between €30 and €40 per day per person on a modest budget, factoring accommodation, food, and basic expenses. Public albergues (pilgrim hostels) are slightly more expensive on this route than on other Camino routes, with beds costing €12-14 per night; private albergues or hostels range from €15 to €20. For accommodation alternatives, small guesthouses and private rooms can cost €30-50 depending on the town and season.

Food expenses vary depending on whether you cook or eat out. Groceries for two meals per day typically cost €8-10 per person, with supermarkets available in almost every town. Eating out at bars/restaurants commonly involves a Menu del Día (set menu) costing around €12, with coffee and snacks costing €1-4. Buying food and preparing meals in albergue kitchens significantly reduces costs.

Additional optional expenses include luggage transfer services (~€7 per day), laundry (€2-5), occasional souvenirs, and entrance fees to cultural sites. Transportation costs to and from the route vary based on your starting point but generally range between €20-50 for regional buses or trains.

A sample budget breakdown for a 9-day, 2-person trip showed:

- Accommodation: €300
- Food & drinks: €260
- Transport & Laundry: €60
- Total: €620 (€34 per person per day).

For those aiming for a more comfortable experience with private rooms and regular dining out, expect daily budgets of €40-70 per person, while luxury options including hotels and private transfers push costs above €80 daily.

Pilgrims should budget accordingly based on their travel style and preferences to manage their expenses smoothly.

Travel Insurance Considerations

Travel insurance is not mandatory for the Vía de la Plata but strongly recommended due to its remote stretches (30+ km without services), elevation challenges, and risks like heatstroke, sprains, or blisters requiring medical evacuation. Essential coverage includes emergency medical care, hospital stays, repatriation, theft of gear/passport, trip cancellation, and hiking/trekking activities. standard policies may exclude "adventure" sports, so verify explicitly. Costs range €0.50-€2/day; EU citizens supplement with EHIC for basic care, but non-EU need full private plans covering pre-existing conditions.

Key Coverage Essentials

Prioritize policies tailored for Camino pilgrims, checking these must-haves:

- **Medical and Repatriation**: Unlimited or high-limit (€100,000+) for accidents, outpatient/inpatient treatment, air ambulance from isolated Extremadura/Galicia.
- **Trip Disruptions**: Cancellation (illness, weather), delays, early return; luggage loss (cover €1,000+ for backpack/gear).
- **Liability and Theft**: Personal liability, stolen Credential/money; sports add-ons for walking 20-30 km/day.
- **Exclusions Watch**: Pre-existing conditions, pandemics, solo sports—declare all upfront.

2

Chapter Two

What to Bring

Essential Gear Checklist

Pilgrims on the Vía de la Plata need gear that prioritizes lightness, durability, and versatility to handle long stages up to 30 km through varied terrain, from Roman ruins to rural paths. Aim for a total pack weight under 8-10 kg excluding water and food to avoid fatigue. Test all items beforehand on training walks.

- **Backpack (35-45L)**: Choose adjustable models like Rab Aeon or similar with hip belt and chest strap for weight distribution. Include a rain cover.
- **Hydration (2L+ capacity)**: Collapsible bottles or bladder; refill at fountains but carry extra for dry stretches like between Los Santos de Maimona and Villafranca de los Barros.
- **Rain Protection**: Breathable jacket (e.g., Marmot) and poncho or lightweight pants; essential year-round, especially in Galicia.
- **Trekking Poles**: Collapsible for stability on uneven ground and descents; reduces knee strain over 1000 km.
- **Headlamp/Flashlight**: With spare batteries for early mornings or alber-

gue power outages.
- **Sleeping Gear**: Lightweight liner or silk sack for albergues; skip full bag in warmer months as many provide blankets.
- **Quick-Dry Towel**: Microfiber like Sea to Summit for body and laundry.
- **Sunglasses, Sun Hat/Buff, Sunscreen**: UV protection against intense Spanish sun.
- **First Aid Basics**: Blister plasters (Compeed), moleskin, antiseptic, tweezers, scissors, painkillers (ibuprofen).
- **Toiletries (minimal)**: Travel toothbrush, toothpaste, Dr. Bronner's soap (doubles for laundry), earplugs, sink plug.
- **Power Bank**: 10,000mAh+ for phone charging on remote stages.
- **Pilgrim Passport (Credencial)**: Obtain in Seville; collect two sellos daily to avoid running out of pages.
- **Money Belt/Secure Pouch**: For cash, cards, ID; small towns often cash-only.
- **Multi-tool/Spork**: Foldable for meals; stainless steel lunch box useful where kitchens lack utensils.
- **Camp Sandals/Flip-Flops**: For rest and showers to air feet.

Clothing for Variable Weather

The Vía de la Plata spans diverse climates from Andalusia's heat to Galicia's damp chill, with elevations causing sudden shifts. Layering with breathable, quick-dry synthetics or merino wool allows adjustments without excess weight. Wash daily in albergues to rotate a minimal set.

Base Layers
These wick moisture during long walks:

- 2-3 moisture-wicking T-shirts (short-sleeve for heat, one long-sleeve for sun and evenings)
- 3 pairs synthetic or merino underwear (quick-dry, anti-odor)
- 3 pairs hiking socks (wool blend for cushioning and blister prevention;

include liner socks if prone to issues)
- Sports bras (2 for women; merino preferred)

Mid Layers

Add warmth for mornings or higher altitudes like Salamanca:

- Lightweight fleece or merino long-sleeve top (packable, versatile for evenings)
- Thermal base layer top and leggings (for cooler months or windy stages)
- Convertible hiking pants (zip-off to shorts for flexibility)

Outer Layers

Protect against rain and wind common year-round:

- Breathable rain jacket (Gore-Tex or similar; packable)
- Rain pants or poncho (lightweight; poncho covers backpack)
- Windproof shell if jacket lacks it

Accessories

Complete protection and comfort:

- Buff or neck gaiter (sun, dust, cold)
- Sun hat with neck flap and warm beanie
- Lightweight gloves for chilly descents
- Sleep shorts or leggings (double as evening wear)

Prioritize tested, seam-sealed items; avoid cotton which retains moisture. Recent pilgrims note extra layers essential for spring/autumn transitions.

Footwear: Choosing the Right Boots or Shoes

Footwear decisions shape your Vía de la Plata experience, as the route mixes flat paved sections, dirt paths, rocky stretches, and occasional steep descents over 1000 km. Prioritize breathability, cushioning, and a wide toe box to handle foot swelling after 20-30 km days. Trail running shoes dominate pilgrim choices for their light weight and quick drying, outperforming heavy boots on this mostly non-technical path.

Recommended Types

- **Trail Running Shoes**: Top pick for most pilgrims; lightweight (under 300g per shoe), flexible, with grippy outsoles for varied terrain. Ideal for the route's heat and flatter profile from Seville to Astorga.
- **Lightweight Hiking Boots**: Low or mid-cut for ankle support on uneven ground near Mérida or Zamora; choose breathable models over stiff high boots.
- **Breathable Hiking Shoes**: Versatile mid-option with reinforced toes and heels; good for spring/fall transitions.
- **Trekking Sandals**: Secondary pair like Keen or Teva for hot days, evenings, or river crossings; not primary due to stone entry on trails.
- **Avoid**: Heavy leather boots (cause fatigue), fully waterproof Gore-Tex in summer (traps heat, blisters), or road runners (poor grip).

Key Brands and Models

Popular, tested options from recent pilgrims:

1. Brand/Model: Hoka Speedgoat/Challenger ATR 5

- Type: Trail Runner
- Key Features: Max cushion, wide toe box, durable outsole
- Best For: Long stages, foot swelling

2. **Brand/Model**: Altra Lone Peak/Olympus 2

- Type: Trail Runner
- Key Features: Zero-drop, roomy fit, lightweight
- Best For: Wide feet, natural gait

3. Brand/Model: Salomon Sense Ultra

- Type: Trail Runner
- Key Features: Secure fit, grip on rocks
- Best For: Mixed terrain, stability

4. Brand/Model: Brooks Cascadia/Ghost

- Type: Trail/Walking
- Key Features: Cushioned, breathable
- Best For: Warm weather, pavement

5. Brand/Model: Merrell Moab

- Type: Hiking Shoe
- Key Features: Supportive, quick-dry
- Best For: Beginners, varied paths

6. Brand/Model: Keen Targhee III

- Type: Low Boot
- Key Features: Ankle protection, blister-free
- Best For: Cooler months

Sizing, Fit, and Care Tips

- Go half to full size up from street shoes for swelling; test with weighted

pack on 20+ km hikes.
- Features: Rubber toe/heel guards, shock absorption, low heel-to-toe drop (4-8mm), padded tongue.
- Break in 50-100 km pre-trip; carry liner socks, Compeed for blisters.
- Rotate pairs if possible; air dry nightly, use newspaper stuffing.

Backpack Selection and Packing Tips

Selecting the right backpack for the Vía de la Plata ensures comfort over 1000 km of varied terrain, from flat Andalusian plains to hilly Castilian stages. Aim for 35-45L capacity to keep total weight under 8-10 kg (excluding water/food), with adjustable torso fit, padded hip belt, and ventilation to transfer 80% of load to hips. Integrated rain cover is essential for sudden showers.

Recommended Backpacks

Popular models tested by recent pilgrims balance capacity, lightness, and features:

1. Brand/Model: Osprey Stratos 36

- Capacity: 36L
- Weight: 1.5 kg
- Key Features: Mesh backpanel, hip pockets, trekking pole attachments, side access
- Best For: All-season comfort

2. Brand/Model: Osprey Exos/Tempest 38

- Capacity: 38L
- Weight: 1.2 kg
- Key Features: Ultralight frame, hydration sleeve, adjustable torso
- Best For: Minimalists, summer

3. Brand/Model: Deuter Futura/Aeon 40

- Capacity: 40L
- Weight: 1.4 kg
- Key Features: Aircontact system, rain cover, organization pockets
- Best For: European pilgrims, variable weather

4. **Brand/Model**: Gregory Citro 30/Paragon 38

- Capacity: 30-38L
- Weight: 1.1 kg
- Key Features: Suspended mesh, hipbelt pockets, top-loader
- Best For: Hot/dry stages, lightweight

5. Brand/Model: Quechua Forclaz 40

- Capacity: 40L
- Weight: 1.3 kg
- Key Features: Affordable, durable, available in Spain
- Best For: Budget, Decathlon shoppers

Fit at a store: torso length 40-50 cm typical; women often need shorter models like Osprey Tempest.

Packing Principles

- **Weight Distribution**: Heavy items (water, food) low/center near spine; light/sleeping bag high. Use hip belt for stability on descents.
- **Organization**: Compression cubes/dry bags for clothes (separate clean/dirty); accessible top pouch for snacks/rain gear; bottom for sleeping items.
- **Daily Capacity**: Leave 20% empty for food (sandwiches on 30+ km stages like Fuentes de Oñoro).

- **Test Run**: Load fully, walk 20 km; adjust straps for no shoulder rub.
- **Maintenance**: Air nightly; repair kit for tears.

Avoid overpacking—start small to force minimalism.

First Aid and Medical Supplies

A compact first aid kit weighing under 300g handles the Vía de la Plata's common issues like blisters from 20-30 km stages, sprains on rocky paths, and dehydration in Extremadura heat. Pharmacies (farmacias) appear every 10-20 km, so focus on basics to bridge gaps; restock in larger towns like Mérida or Salamanca. Personalize for allergies or conditions, and learn blister drainage technique.

Blister Prevention and Treatment

Blisters top pilgrim complaints; prevent with fitted shoes, wool socks, and foot powder.

1. Item: Compeed/Blister Plasters

    - Purpose: Cushion and heal hot spots/blisters
    - Quantity/Tips: 6-10; apply over intact skin

2. Item: Moleskin or Leukotape

    - Purpose: Prevent rubbing; tape toes/heels
    - Quantity/Tips: Roll; cut to fit, use with tincture of benzoin

3. Item: Sterile Needles/Thread

    - Purpose: Drain large blisters safely
    - Quantity/Tips: 2-3; disinfect, leave skin intact

4. Item: Foot Powder/Vaseline

- Purpose: Reduce friction, dry feet
- Quantity/Tips: Small tub; nightly application

Wound Care and Antiseptics

Clean minor cuts from thorns or falls promptly to avoid infection.

- Antiseptic wipes/cream (alcohol, iodine, chlorhexidine): Disinfect wounds
- Assorted plasters/bandages: Cover abrasions
- Sterile gauze and hypoallergenic tape: Larger wounds
- Latex gloves/hand sanitizer: Safe treatment

Pain Relief and Medications

Manage aches without over-relying; Spanish brands like Paracetamol match generics.

- Ibuprofen/paracetamol (400mg/500mg): Pain, inflammation, headaches
- Antihistamines: Allergies, bites
- Anti-inflammatory gel (Voltaren): Muscle strains
- Prescription meds: 2-week supply + note
- Electrolyte tablets: Dehydration prevention

Tools and Miscellaneous

- Small scissors/tweezers: Bandage work, splinters, nails
- Elastic bandages: Sprains, compression
- Insect repellent: Summer mosquitoes

Store in waterproof pouch; check expiry dates.

What to Leave at Home

Leaving non-essentials behind keeps your Vía de la Plata pack under 10 kg, preventing fatigue on 30 km stages through Extremadura plains or Galician hills. Spain's frequent shops, pharmacies, and albergues supply replacements, so resist "just in case" items that add weight without value. Pilgrims regret heavy loads most, as lighter packs enable faster recovery and enjoyment.

Heavy or Bulky Items

Skip gear available along the route or that burdens long walks:

- Full sleeping bag: Albergues provide blankets; silk liner suffices
- Heavy towels: Microfiber quick-dry versions only
- Multiple shoes/boots: One primary pair + camp sandals
- Laptop/tablet: Phone handles navigation/photos

Excess Clothing and Toiletries

Minimalism rules; wash nightly and buy as needed:

- Cotton clothes/jeans: Retain moisture, cause chafing
- Multiple outfits: 2-3 shirts, 3 underwear/socks rotate
- Full-size toiletries: Travel minis or solid bars
- Extra layers beyond fleece/rain jacket: Layer smartly

Unnecessary Gadgets and Misc

Tech and extras tempt but drain battery/weight:

- Earphones/chess sets/poker chips: Unused distractions
- Excessive electronics/chargers: One power bank covers phone
- "Emergency" food: Markets daily; carry day's snacks
- Valuables/jewelry: Theft risk low but minimalize

Test pack on 20 km walks; ditch anything unused.

3

Chapter Three

Logistics and Practicalities

Getting to Seville (or Your Starting Point)

Seville serves as the traditional Vía de la Plata start, with its international airport (SVQ) offering direct flights from Europe and Spain. Fly via Ryanair, Vueling, EasyJet, or Iberia (€20-50 if early); trains/buses from Madrid or Barcelona provide alternatives. Rest a day pre-walk to acclimate and collect your Credencial at the cathedral.

From Major Cities
 Efficient connections make Seville accessible

1. Origin: Madrid (MAD)

- Option: Flight
- Time: 1h10m
- Cost (€): 30+
- Notes: Barajas to SVQ

2. Origin: Madrid

    - Option: AVE Train
    - Time: 2h40m
    - Cost (€): 40+
    - Notes: Puerta de Atocha

3. Origin: Madrid

    - Option: Bus
    - Time: 6h20m
    - Cost (€): 25-34
    - Notes: ALSA/Socibus

4. Origin: Barcelona

    - Option: Flight
    - Time: 1h45m
    - Cost (€): 31+
    - Notes: Ryanair/Vueling

5. Origin: Barcelona

    - Option: Train
    - Time: 5h30m-11h30m
    - Cost (€): 65-120
    - Notes: No direct bus

6. Origin: Porto

    - Option: Bus
    - Time: 6-8h
    - Cost (€): 20-30

- Notes: ALSA

To Seville City Center and Camino Start

SVQ airport: C1 bus (€4, 35min) or taxi (€22-30) to cathedral. Walk starts at Seville Cathedral's north door on Avenida de la Constitución—follow tram tracks to Calle Zaragoza, then Puerta de Triana bridge over Guadalquivir. Yellow arrows guide urban exit to Guillena (23 km).

Alternative Starting Points

Skip initial heat/urban stages if short on time:

- **Mérida** (Stage 6 end, 160 km from Seville): ALSA bus from Seville (€6-9, 2h); Roman ruins hub.
- **Cáceres** (more historic): Bus/train from Seville/Madrid.
- **Salamanca/Ourense**: For final 100/200 km qualifying for Compostela; fly to closer airports.
- **Zafra**: Midway, good for testing.

These shorten the full 1000 km route while hitting highlights.

Getting Home from Santiago de Compostela

Santiago de Compostela (SCQ airport, 10 km out) offers flights across Europe/Spain; buses/trains connect efficiently to Madrid, Porto, or back south. Collect your Compostela first at the Pilgrim Office (Rúa do Vilar 1, open 10am-8pm peak season), carry passport and Credential. Plan 1-2 rest days post-walk amid celebrations.

Airport Transfers

SCQ handles Ryanair, Vueling, Iberia; taxis (€25, 20min), private shuttles (€9-15/person), or Line 6A bus (€1.50, 25min) to center/airport. Direct flights to Seville (1h45m, €30+), Madrid (1h20m, €25+).

To Major Destinations

1. Destination: Madrid (MAD Airport)

   - Option: Flight
   - Time: 1h20m
   - Cost (€): 25-60
   - Notes: Ryanair/Iberia direct

2. Destination: Madrid

   - Option: AVE Train
   - Time: 3h-3h30m
   - Cost (€): 50-120
   - Notes: Chamartín station

3. Destination: Madrid

   - Option: Bus
   - Time: 9h30m-10h
   - Cost (€): 52-95
   - Notes: ALSA direct to T4 airport

4. Destination: Seville

   - Option: Flight
   - Time: 1h45m
   - Cost (€): 30-70
   - Notes: Via Vueling; connect from SCQ

5. Destination: Seville

   - Option: Bus
   - Time: 12h+

- Cost (€): 50+
- Notes: Changes in Ourense/Merida

6. Destination: Porto (OPO)

- Option: Bus
- Time: 3h
- Cost (€): 15-25
- Notes: Flixbus/ALSA

7. Destination: Ourense

- Option: Bus/Train
- Time: 1h30m-2h
- Cost (€): 8-15
- Notes: Frequent for Sanabrés variant

Tips for Smooth Departure

- Validate Compostela before flights (digital copy via email).
- Luggage: ALSA 25kg free; excess €10-20. Train 30kg.
- Peak summer: Book 2-4 weeks ahead; off-season flexible.
- Taxi to Lavacolla (end of walk) if needed (€15).
- Return loop: Fly home or bus/train reverse route via Salamanca.

Pilgrims note trains most scenic/comfortable; airport buses align with flights.

Credential and Compostela: What You Need to Know

The Credencial (pilgrim passport) grants discounted albergue access and proves your journey for the Compostela certificate at Santiago. Buy one (or two for full route stamps) early; collect 2 stamps daily from albergues, churches, bars. Present stamped Credential at Santiago's Pilgrim Office for validation; spiritual motive required.

Obtaining the Credencial

Start in Seville at official spots; €2 cost supports maintenance.

1. Location: Seville

   - Where: Amigos del Camino (Calle Castilla 82, Triana)

2. Location: Seville

   - Where: Hotel Simón or Triana Backpackers
   - Hours/Notes: Convenient near start

3. Location: Later Towns

   - Where: Municipal albergues (Zamora, Zafra)
   - Hours/Notes: €2; available mid-route

4. Location: General

   - Where: Churches, associations, Correos online
   - Hours/Notes: Free/donation at some; 54-stamp capacity

Buy extras for 1000 km—protect in plastic sleeve.

Collecting Stamps (Sellos)

Stamps validate distance; seek unique designs.

- **Daily Rule**: 1-2 stamps/day; churches (free), albergues (check-in), cafés (€ purchase often).
- **Locations**: Bars, shops, ayuntamientos; rural Vía de la Plata has fewer—ask ¿Sello, por favor? .

- **Final 100 km**: Strictly 2/day reviewed for Compostela.
- **Tips**: Morning stamps prevent shortages; photocopy Credential as backup.

Compostela Requirements

Issued free at Pilgrim Office (Rúa Carretas 33, Santiago); arrive post-Cathedral.

1. Means: Foot/Horse

   - Minimum Distance: Last 100 km to Cathedral
   - Vía de la Plata Specifics: Full route qualifies; prove via stamps

2. Means: Bike

   - Minimum Distance: Last 200 km
   - Vía de la Plata Specifics: Same stamping rule

3. Means: Boat/Wheelchair

   - Minimum Distance: Case-by-case
   - Vía de la Plata Specifics: 100 nautical miles + foot finish

Spiritual/religious motive declaration; non-qualifiers get Welcome Certificate.

Common Pitfalls and Tips

- Lose Credential? Buy replacement, note prior stamps.
- Groups: Individual presentation preferred.
- Digital? No—physical only.
- Storage: Frame or scan post-journey.

Pilgrims emphasize early Credential purchase and diligent stamping for seamless Compostela.

Accommodation Options: Albergues, Hotels, and Hostels

The Vía de la Plata offers 60+ albergues across its stages, supplemented by hotels and hostels in larger towns like Seville, Zafra, and Salamanca. Public albergues prioritize pilgrims with Credential (first-come, 8pm curfew common); private options provide more comfort. Expect €10-15/night for dorms, €30-60 for privates; book ahead in summer.

Albergues (Pilgrim Hostels)
Primary lodging: bunk beds, shared facilities, communal vibe.

1. Type: Municipal (Public)

   - Price (€): 10-14
   - Features: Basic, pilgrim-only, Credencial required
   - Examples: Tábara (must-stay, historic), Zafra Convento

2. Type: Private

   - Price (€): 12-20
   - Features: Kitchens, WiFi, laundry (€2-3), pools
   - Examples: El Zaguán de la Plata (Zafra, garden/pool), Hervás old station

3. Type: Donativo (Donation)

   - Price (€): Voluntary
   - Features: Rare, community-run
   - Examples: Occasional in Extremadura

Arrive by 2pm; some close seasonally

Hotels and Pensions

Private rooms for privacy; often cheaper than cities.

- **Budget Pensions/Hostales**: €25-40 single, €40-60 double; breakfast included sometimes (e.g., Hostal Asturias near Jarilla, Hostal el Monte).
- **Mid-Range Hotels**: €50-80; amenities like restaurants (Hotel La Fábrica, Hotel Jarilla).
- **Chain Options**: Eurostars Vía de la Plata (Astorga), Alda Vía de la Plata (La Bañeza).

Hostels (Urban/Seville Focus)

Backpacker-style in Seville (no public albergue); social, mixed guests.

1. Hostel: Toc Hostel Sevilla

   - Location: Center
   - Price (€): 20-30
   - Notes: Kitchen, tapas bar

2. Hostel: Triana Backpackers

   - Location: Triana
   - Price (€): 15-25
   - Notes: Credencial available, lively

3. Hostel: The Spot Central

   - Location: Seville
   - Price (€): 20-30
   - Notes: Clean, central

Less common mid-route; use for rest days.

Booking Strategy: When to Reserve Ahead

Public albergues on the Vía de la Plata operate first-come-first-served—no reservations allowed, requiring early arrivals (by 2pm) to secure beds. Private albergues, hotels, and hostels accept bookings, essential during peaks when capacity fills fast on fixed stages like Castilblanco-Almadén. Flexibility varies by season and town size.

By Season and Demand

Tailor strategy to timing; Vía de la Plata sees fewer pilgrims than Frances but rural limits amplify crowds.

1. Season: Peak (Jun-Sep, Easter, Jubilee)

    - Booking Need: High—book privates/hotels 1-4 weeks ahead
    - Strategy: Reserve key stages (Zafra, Salamanca weekends); walk-ins risky

2. Season: Shoulder (Apr-May, Oct)

    - Booking Need: Medium—1-2 weeks for privates
    - Strategy: Public OK if early; monitor via apps

3. Season: Low (Nov-Mar)

    - Booking Need: Low—walk-ins suffice
    - Strategy: Closures common; confirm openings

Accommodation Type Rules

1. Type: Public Albergues

    - Reservations? No

- Tips: Credential required; arrive early, €12-14

2. Type: Private Albergues/Hostels

   - Reservations? Yes
   - Tips: €15-20; kitchens/WiFi; book via site/phone

3. Type: Hotels/Pensions

   - Reservations? Yes
   - Tips: €40+

Tools and Best Practices

- **Hybrid Approach**: Book 1-2 days ahead for privates; public for flexibility. Groups/families prioritize hotels.
- **Rural Caution**: Long stages (e.g., 40 km gaps) have 1-2 options—pre-check closures
- **Cancellations**: Flexible policies; notify if deviating.

Pilgrims report no issues off-peak without bookings, but Easter/peak requires planning to avoid 10+ km walks to alternatives.

Food and Water Along the Route

Food and water on the Vía de la Plata follow the route's rhythm—plentiful in villages with albergues, sparse on rural stretches up to 30 km long. Every town has a supermarket or bar for basics like bread, cheese, and fruit, but long stages demand planning. Carry at least 2 liters of water and high-energy snacks like nuts or energy bars to bridge gaps between services. Pilgrim menus (€10-15) pop up occasionally in larger towns such as Zafra or Salamanca, typically offering three courses with a drink at Spanish hours: lunch around 2pm and dinner near 9pm.

Start your day with a solid breakfast at a bar—think coffee, toast with jamón, and fresh orange juice (€3-5)—before tackling stretches without facilities. Bocadillos (filled baguettes, €3-5) from cafés make perfect trail lunches, paired with supermarket finds like yogurt or bananas. Many private albergues have kitchens where you can cook pasta or heat microwave meals, a lifesaver when bars close early or on Mondays. For dinner, scan for Menú del peregrino signs, but self-catering sustains you through smaller villages.

Water comes from reliable village fountains in plazas or near churches, often marked safe for drinking—though always check for agua no potable warnings and boil if unsure. Bars gladly refill bottles for free, and bottled water (€1 per liter) sells everywhere. Critical dry sections like Castilblanco de los Barros to Almadén de la Plata (30 km with nothing) or Los Santos de Maimona to Villafranca de los Barros (15 km, no shade) require full hydration from the start. Add electrolyte tablets to combat summer heat, especially in Extremadura.

Regional specialties add flavor to your journey: try jamón ibérico and queso manchego in Extremadura, hearty lentejas estofadas in Castile, or pulpo a la gallega as you near Galicia. Vegans and gluten-free travelers should stock specialty items early, as options thin out rurally. Daily food costs run €15-25 excluding albergues, with 4000-6000 calories needed for 20-30 km days.

Language Basics: Essential Spanish Phrases

Mastering basic Spanish transforms the Vía de la Plata from a solitary trek into a tapestry of connections, as rural albergues, family-run mesonés, and isolated villagers along its 1,000 km often speak little English—especially outside Seville, Salamanca, or León. Pilgrims report warmer welcomes, better deals (e.g., €2 off a menú del día), and insider tips like unmarked water fountains or evening mass times when using phrases, even with accents; locals appreciate the effort, often responding in simpler Spanish or gestures. Practice via apps like Duolingo's Camino-specific playlists, focusing on polite, slow pronunciation—record yourself saying Buen Camino (bwen kah-MEE-no) to nail the rolling 'r'. Time investment: 30 minutes daily pre-trip yields

CHAPTER THREE

80% comprehension in daily interactions; carry a pocket phrasebook or Google Translate offline for backups.

Core Greetings and Politeness

These open doors everywhere—from dawn hellos at albergue check-ins to sunset chats over tapas—building rapport that leads to shared wine or route advice.

- Hola (OH-la): Hello/hi, universal icebreaker for pilgrims or shopkeepers.
- Buenos días (BWEH-nos DEE-as): Good morning, until noonish; shifts to Buenas tardes (BWEH-nas TAR-des) post-siesta (2-5 p.m.).
- Buenas noches (BWEH-nas NOH-ches): Good evening/night, from dusk; doubles as "goodbye" late.
- Adiós (ah-dee-OHS) or Hasta luego (AHS-tah LWEH-go): Bye/see you later.
- Gracias (GRAH-see-ahs): Thank you; reply De nada (deh NAH-da), you're welcome.
- Por favor (por fah-VOR): Please, softens any request.
- Perdón/Disculpe (pehr-DOHN/dees-KOOL-peh): Excuse me/sorry, vital for crowded plazas or trail passes.
- Buen Camino (bwen kah-MEE-no): Pilgrim's greeting/wish for "good walk"—say it passing anyone; response is mutual or ¡Ultreia! (ool-TRAY-ah, onward!).

Navigation and Trail Essentials

The Vía's arrows fade on rural stretches (e.g., Extremadura plains), so these phrases locate yellow shells, avoid N-roads, or flag rides—pilgrims save hours asking locals.

- ¿Dónde está el Camino? (DOHN-deh ehs-tah el kah-MEE-no): Where's the Camino?
- ¿Cómo llego a...? (KOH-mo YEH-go ah): How do I get to...? (e.g., albergue, farmacia).

- Derecha (deh-REH-cha): Right; Izquierda (ees-kee-EHR-da): Left; Recto (rehk-TOH): Straight.
- ¿Está lejos? (ehs-TAH leh-HOHS): Is it far?; ¿Hay agua/cajero cerca? (AH-ee AH-gwa/ka-HEH-ro SEHR-ka): Water/ATM nearby?
- Estoy perdido/a (ehs-TOY pehr-DEE-do/ah): I'm lost (add gender).
- ¿Seville/Astorga/Salamanca? for town names; point to map app.

Accommodations and Pilgrim Credentials

Secure beds in low-season albergues (donativo €5-10) or negotiate private rooms (€20-35) with these—mention peregrino status for priority.

- ¿Tiene cama libre para peregrino? (TYEH-neh KAH-ma LEE-bray pah-rah peh-reh-GREE-no): Pilgrim bed free?
- Quisiera una cama/cena (kee-see-EH-rah OO-na KAH-ma/SEH-na): I'd like a bed/dinner.
- ¿Cuánto cuesta? (KWAHN-toh KWEHS-ta): How much?; ¿Más barato? (mahs bah-RAH-to): Cheaper?
- ¿Sello en la credencial? (SEH-yo en lah kre-dehn-SYAL): Stamp in credential? (Show pilgrim passport).
- ¿Abre a las...? (AH-breh ahs las): Opens at...?; note siesta closures.

Food, Drink, and Shopping

Fuel 25 km days with affordable menús (€10-15); specify needs to avoid surprises in meat-heavy regions like Castilla y León.

- ¿Menú del día? (meh-NOO del DEE-ah): Daily menu/special.
- Una cerveza/vino por favor (OO-na sehr-VEH-sa/VEE-no): A beer/wine please.
- Soy vegetariano/a (soy veh-heh-tah-ree-AH-no/ah): I'm vegetarian; Sin gluten/lactosa (seen GLOO-ten/lahk-TOH-sa): No gluten/lactose.
- ¿Alérgico a nueces/mariscos? (ah-LEHR-hee-ko ah NWEH-kes/mahr-EES-kos): Allergic to nuts/seafood?
- ¿Pan/agua/botella? (pahn/AH-gwa/bo-TEH-ya): Bread/water/bottle?;

¿Cuánto es? for prices.
- Regional: Tortilla española (potato omelet), Caldo gallego (Galician soup), Jamón (ham—ubiquitous).

Health, Emergencies, and Numbers

Remote stages (e.g., Mérida-Salamanca) lack pharmacies; these bridge gaps until towns.

- ¿Dónde está la farmacia/hospital? (fahr-MAH-see-ah/ohs-pee-TAHL): Pharmacy/hospital?
- ¿Farmacia abierta? (ah-BEHR-ta): Pharmacy open? (Few Sundays).
- Me duele la...pPierna/rodilla/pie (MEH DWEH-leh lah PEHR-na/ro-DEE-ya/pee): My leg/knee/foot hurts (blisters common).
- ¡Ayuda!/¡Socorro! (ah-YOO-da/so-KOH-rro): Help!
- Numbers: Uno (OO-no:1), Dos (dohs:2), up to Diez (dee-EHS:10); count kilometers or change.

Regional Variations and Pronunciation Tips

Vía spans Andalusia (Sevilla lisps 'c/z' as 'th'), Extremadura (rural drawl), Castilla (crisp), Galicia (softer, Celtic influence)—Gracias stays universal. Stress final syllables; roll 'r' lightly; women add -a endings. Practice with YouTube "Camino Spanish" videos or apps; locals correct kindly. Beyond basics, learn town names: Aljucén , Zamora .

Money Matters: ATMs, Cards, and Cash

Carry €200-300 cash upon arrival, as municipal/donativo albergues (€5-15), rural bars, and small shops demand it—cards fail 20-30% of stops, especially Extremadura's plains or Galician hamlets where ATMs vanish for 50-100 km. Daily needs (€30-50) split 70% card (hotels, supermarkets in Seville/Salamanca) and 30% cash (pilgrim meals, buses); post-2023 regulations cap cash payments at €1,000 but pilgrims rarely hit limits. Notify banks pre-trip to avoid blocks; Revolut/Wise debit cards minimize 1-3%

foreign fees over traditional ATM pulls (€2-5 each).

ATMs: Locations and Reliability

ATMs cluster in towns every 20-40 km but skip remote stages—stock up in Seville, Mérida, Zafra, Salamanca, Zamora, Astorga before voids like Cañaveral-Montamarta (no ATM, 28 km).

- **Seville to Mérida (first 200 km)**: Abundant at airports, stations; roadside at A-66 services (e.g., 10 km pre-Almendralejo).
- **Extremadura (Mérida-Zafra)**: Zafra, Puebla de Sancho Pérez, Calzadilla de los Barros; scarce in hamlets—pull €100+.
- **Castilla y León (Salamanca-Astorga)**: Reliable in Salamanca, Zamora; Alija del Infantado, La Bañeza; gaps near Granja de Moreruela.
- **Galicia (Sanabrés/Ourense-Santiago)**: Ourense last pre-90 km stretch; Finisterre variants spotty.

Withdraw €100-200 per hit from bank-affiliated machines (BBVA, CaixaBank) during hours (9am-2pm Mon-Fri, some Sat); avoid independents charging €5+ fees.

Cards: Best Options and Pitfalls

Visa/Mastercard dominate; bring 2 debit + 1 credit (e.g., Revolut for 0% fees, no FX markup) plus Apple Pay backup—tap works in 80% larger spots but glitches on older terminals. Chip+PIN mandatory (no swipe); US cards notify issuers or risk freezes. Private albergues/hotels (€20-40) accept 90%, but donativos cash-only; test in Seville. Limits: €300-500 daily; split across cards.

1. Card Type: Revolut/Wise Debit

- Pros: 0% fees, app controls, instant top-up
- Cons: Daily limits €200-400
- Vía Suitability: Ideal for pilgrims

2. Card Type: Bank Debit (Visa)

- Pros: Widespread
- Cons: 1-3% FX + €2-5 ATM
- Vía Suitability: Backup, notify travel

3. Card Type: Credit (Amex rare)

- Pros: Rewards, purchase protection
- Cons: Declines in villages, cash advance fees
- Vía Suitability: Cities only

Daily Budget Breakdown and Tips

€30-40/day baseline: €10 albergue, €12 menú, €5 snacks/beer, €3 misc—scale to €50+ for privates.

- **Cash-heavy**: Albergues (donativo envelope), bar tabs, buses (€5-10 Seville-Mérida), market fruit.
- **Card-friendly**: Supermercados (Mercadona), larger mesonés, pharmacies.

Start with €250 euros (airport exchange poor—ATM instead); divide wallets (one hidden). Track via app; tip €1-2 meals for goodwill. Theft rare but use money belts; photocopy cards.

Emergencies and Long-Term Strategy

Lost card? Embassy aid slow—carry passport copy, secondary cards in separate pack. Budget €1,200-1,800/40 days excluding flights; Galicia inflates with rain gear. Pre-load multi-currency apps; exchange excess in Santiago (banks open). This system ensures fluid 1,000 km flow, dodging money stress for pure pilgrimage focus.

4

Chapter Four

Health and Safety

Common Injuries and How to Prevent Them

Blisters top the list for Vía de la Plata walkers, forming from sweat-soaked feet rubbing in hot southern stages or ill-fitting boots on gravel paths. They slow you down fast if infected, especially on long hauls without services. Break them in over 100 km at home, layer thin liner socks under merino wool, and tape hot spots with Leukotape before they pop; carry Compeed and antiseptic for fixes.

Knee pain and patellar tendonitis strike on endless downhills from backpack sway and weak quads, making each step a grind by week two. Trekking poles cut joint load by 25 percent, so grip them firm on descents. Strengthen with squats and lunges pre-trip, ice nightly with a frozen bottle, and lighten your pack to under 10 percent of body weight.

Shin splints burn along the front of your lower legs from pounding hard-packed roads and sudden mileage jumps. They flare early for couch-to-Camino folks. Switch to cushioned trail shoes, stretch calves gently after walks, and ice for 15 minutes daily to calm inflammation.

Ankle sprains happen on loose rocks and ruts in Extremadura's dry terrain, twisting you off course mid-stage. Slow down on uneven spots, plant wide steps, and wear supportive mids or braces if history bites. Elevate and wrap immediately if it rolls.

Achilles tendonitis creeps from tight calves on uphills, swelling overnight after 30 km days. Do eccentric heel drops daily to rebuild it tough. Rest at first twinge, avoid hill bombs, and massage with arnica gel.

Plantar fasciitis stabs your heel first thing mornings from flat arches on concrete stretches. Roll a frozen water bottle underfoot each night. Get orthotic insoles if prone, and stretch toes upward holding for 30 seconds.

IT band syndrome tightens outer thighs from uneven paths, shooting pain down to knees. Foam roll nightly, strengthen hips with clamshells, and shorten strides on camber roads.

Lower back strain hits from heavy packs or slouching fatigue. Core planks build stability. Adjust waist belt high, keep pack snug, and stretch cat-cow poses at breaks.

Muscle strains pull in calves or hamstrings from cold starts or overreach. Warm up with marches, hold big strides on flats. RICE method heals most in days.

Dealing with Blisters

Blisters plague just about every pilgrim on the Vía de la Plata, popping up from sweaty feet sliding in boots during those scorching southern stages or from gravel grinding toes on long, remote stretches. They start as hot spots under calluses or between toes, then fill with fluid and turn red if you ignore them, risking infection that sidelines you for days in the middle of nowhere. On this Camino, with sparse pharmacies between towns like Almadén de la Plata and Monesterio, catching them early keeps you walking instead of hitchhiking to a doctor.

Feel a burn or rub? Stop right there, peel off your shoe and sock, and dry the spot gently with a clean cloth or tissue from your pack. Slap on a preventive patch like Leukotape or Micropore over the hotspot, sticky side down with a bit of tension for that locked-in feel, then slide your foot back into a fresh liner sock under your wool pair to wick moisture away all day. Keep changing socks midday at any stream or fountain, airing feet for 10 minutes to let skin breathe and toughen up naturally over the first week.

If a blister forms anyway, don't pop it unless it's huge and rubbing raw; let clear fluid protect the skin underneath like nature intended. For intact ones, cover with hydrocolloid dressings like Compeed or Spenco Second Skin, which draw out fluid and cushion without sticking to the wound, changing them only when they turn white and sloppy after 24 hours. Popped blisters need cleaning with soap and boiled fountain water or Betadine, then a light layer of antibiotic ointment like Neosporin under a fresh dressing, wrapped snug but not tourniquet-tight to fight off dirt from those dusty paths.

Your blister kit stays light at 100 grams: 20 Compeed patches, roll of Leukotape with scissors, antiseptic wipes, needle sterilized over a lighter flame for draining if needed, and moleskin donuts to float pressure off heels. Test socks and shoes on 50 km training walks beforehand, picking seamless toes and roomy toe boxes, since narrow fits spell doom by stage three. Feet swell a full size by afternoon, so lace loose up top and tape pinky toes prone to rubbing against neighbors.

Nightly routine seals the deal: soak feet in cool water with Epsom salts from a farmacia, file down thick skin with a pumice stone gently, and massage in foot cream to soften calluses without weakening them. If pus shows yellow or streaks run red up your leg, that's infection; hobble to the next town's centro de salud for antibiotics and skip ahead by bus to avoid spreading it in crowded albergues. Most blisters fade after 10 days as skin hardens, but solo walkers tape religiously to push through unscathed.

Heat and Sun Protection

The Vía de la Plata bakes under relentless Spanish sun from Seville north through Extremadura, where summer temps climb past 40°C on exposed plains, turning 25 km stages into sweat-drenched battles that drop even fit walkers with heat exhaustion. Dehydration sneaks up fast on those endless olive groves with few fountains, while UV rays scorch necks and arms unprotected by midday, leading to painful burns or worse, sunstroke that lands you in a hospital bed instead of an albergue. Spring and fall offer milder 20-30°C days, but southern heat demands respect year-round, especially solo on remote stretches like Almadén de la Plata to Monesterio.

Start walking at first light around 6 AM when shadows stretch long across fields, knocking out 15 km before noon heat peaks, then hole up in shade for siesta till 4 PM when it dips enough to finish strong. Chug water constantly from two 1-liter bottles refilled at every village tap—aim for 4-5 liters daily, mixing in electrolyte tabs like Nuun or sea salt packets to replace what pours out in sweat, since plain water flushes minerals and cramps hit hard. Wear loose long-sleeve shirts in light colors, a legionnaire hat with neck flap, and buff around your throat to block 95 percent of rays; buff sleeves zip on over arms for quick cover when sun climbs high.

Slather broad-spectrum SPF 50 cream thick on face, ears, hands every two hours, even under clothing, and pop a lip balm with zinc for that constant smack against dry wind. Trekking poles double as sun shields when planted ahead, and wide-brim hats beat baseball caps for all-around shade on treeless paths. Watch your crew: dizziness, nausea, pounding head, or dark urine scream heat issues—sit in shade, sip salted broth from a bar, and cool with wet bandana till color returns to cheeks.

Pack smart with a mini umbrella for instant portable shade on brutal days, cooling towels soaked and wrung out at fountains to drape neck and wrists, and frozen bandanas twisted tight for that icy hug mid-morning. Avoid black packs that suck heat; go light colors with reflective space blankets folded small for emergency shade setups. In albergues, hang laundry to dry fast and sleep with fan pointed at feet to drop core temp overnight.

Night drops cool quick up north, but southern stages stay warm; layer a windbreaker for chills after sweat dries. If thunderheads build, seek solid shelter fast since flash floods rip through dry riverbeds. Acclimatize two weeks pre-trip with hot afternoon walks at home to train your body, and never push a stage hungover or jet-lagged—heat amplifies every weakness.

Wildlife and Natural Hazards

The Vía de la Plata threads through diverse landscapes where nature's surprises await, but serious wildlife threats are rare. Most common encounters are with farm dogs guarding fields and flocks, who bark fiercely but usually avoid biting if you stay calm and keep moving. A firm voice, waving trekking poles, or dropping a rock behind you wards them off quickly. Sheep, goats, and cattle occasionally block narrow paths, demanding patience but no real danger.

Watch your step for snakes, especially in dry, rocky scrubland through Extremadura. Spanish vipers tend to avoid humans but may sun themselves on stones or cinder pathways. Never stick hands or feet blindly in bushes or under rocks, and shake out shoes before putting them on at camp to avoid unpleasant surprises. Scorpions hide beneath logs or stones, so avoid sitting or resting directly on the ground without checking first.

Natural hazards include sudden weather changes—storm clouds can build quickly in the mountains of Galicia, turning trails slick with rain and making river crossings more dangerous. Flash floods lurk in dry riverbeds (ramblas) common in southern sections after heavy rain; never cross swollen waters, find higher ground and wait for conditions to clear. Loose gravel and worn stone pathways challenge footing, so use poles and watch for slipped rocks, especially on descents outside towns.

For walking safety, stick to marked trails even if detours look tempting, especially in remote areas where phone signal drops. Wildlife poses minimal risk when respecting distance and moving calmly, but always carry a whistle or small horn to scare off animals if needed and alert fellow trekkers.

Walking Alone vs. in Groups

The Vía de la Plata lets you choose: walk alone or with others. Both are safe and popular. Many pilgrims do one or both. The route is quiet with few people. This makes it good for thinking or sharing stories. Pick what matches your style. You can switch anytime.

CHAPTER FOUR

Why Walk Alone?

Walking solo gives freedom. You go at your speed. No waiting for slow friends. Use the time to think deep thoughts. See sunrises over empty fields near Mérida. Hear birds and wind only. Pilgrims say it builds strength. You face small problems like rain or hills alone. This grows confidence. A 76-year-old woman walked it solo in 2025. She felt safe. Solo women often report no issues. The Camino code helps: pilgrims greet and watch out for each other. But long empty parts exist, like 25km from Fuente de Cantos with no shops. Plan water and food. Finish before dark. Share your day's stops with family via WhatsApp.

Why Walk in Groups?

Groups add fun and help. Meet at albergues in Zafra or Salamanca. Walk 20-30km together. Share maps, snacks, and laughs. Split costs for taxis on bad weather days. Watch each other's packs from thieves. Help with blisters or tired legs. Talk about life over coffee. Groups motivate on hard days like climbs near Lubián. A group once carried an injured friend to a health center. Organized tours handle bookings. But groups mean less freedom. Match speeds or argue. Slow people hold back fast ones. Set rules early: take turns leading, rest together.

Pros and Cons Side by Side

Solo Pros:

- Your own pace and stops.
- Quiet time for prayer or podcasts.
- Meet people your way at bars.
- Full control of your path.

Solo Cons:

- Lonely on rainy days.
- Carry all your own gear.

- No one to share emergencies.

Group Pros:

- Safety in numbers.
- Shared costs and tasks.
- More stories and friends.
- Help for injuries fast.

Group Cons:

- Slower if speeds differ.
- Less alone time.
- Group fights possible.
- Harder to change plans.

Most pilgrims mix: solo mornings, group afternoons. This gets the best of both. The route has low crime. Stick to yellow arrows. Walk in daylight.

Tips for Solo Walkers

- Walk dawn to dusk. No dark starts unless with light.
- One earbud only for music.
- Drink only what you buy or pour.
- Stop at bars—ask about path ahead.
- Pair up for industrial areas near towns.
- Check feet daily for blisters.
- Use pilgrim credential—it shows you're real.

Tips for Group Walkers

- Pick same fitness level.
- Share one first-aid kit.

- Rotate who checks arrows.
- Plan rest days together.
- Vote on changes.
- Help weak links—no one left behind.
- Eat as a team for strength.

Solo or group, the Vía changes you. Quiet paths teach inside. Friends add joy. Say ¡Buen Camino! and go.

Safety Tips for Solo Travelers

Look, walking the Vía de la Plata alone is no big deal. I've read tons of pilgrim stories—solo women, older folks, everyone does it. Locals love pilgrims; they point out arrows and share coffee. Rural cops patrol too. Just be smart, and you'll be fine.

Plan each day simple. Text family your start and end points every morning. Use the AlertCops app—one tap sends your location to police. Aim for 20-25km stages, done by 4pm. No walking after dark, especially in fall when it gets black quick. Check weather; sit out storms in a town like Zafra. On dry stretches like Monterrubio, carry 3 liters water and snacks from the last shop.

Pack right. Keep your backpack 8-10kg. Get one with locks for zips. Wear a day pouch up front for phone and cash. Whistle around your neck, headlamp for dusk, power bank always. Download Maps.me with the Vía route offline. Your pilgrim credential is gold—shows you're legit. Basic first aid: plasters, savlon, ibuprofen. Pepper spray's legal; EU SIM for cheap calls.

On the trail, stick to yellow arrows—no wandering. Earbud in one ear only so you hear bikes coming. Say ¡Buen Camino! or Buenos días! to everyone. Stops at bars for latest path gossip—ask ¿Hay algún problema adelante? (Any trouble ahead?). Team up quick for road sections near Salamanca. Check feet morning and night; blisters kill solo trips. Drink bottled water or filter streams.

In towns, lock your stuff. Passport copy in bag, real one safe. €50 cash daily, cards for big buys. Busy albergues first—hospitaleros vet people. Valuables under pillow or in sleeping bag. Ladies, private room if you want one, €15-25. Don't drink solo at night; eat with the crowd. Facebook's Via de la Plata Pilgrims group is gold for real-time advice.

Animals? Dogs bark loud but back off if you wave a stick and walk steady. Ticks hide in grass—tuck pants in socks, check legs at night. Snakes sun themselves on hot rocks—step wide. Cyclists yell when passing. Dodgy drunk? Smile, keep moving. Guardia Civil's your friend—dial 062 for anything. Solo women say from Mérida to Santiago, smooth sailing.

Health-wise, get insurance with evac cover. EU folks, grab EHIC. Eat protein to fight tiredness. Take rest days in Plasencia. Feeling lonely? Chat at dinner. Podcasts kill empty miles. Journal your thoughts. One pilgrim put it perfect: "Solo made me strong, never scared." That's the Vía magic.

Do this stuff, and you're set. Walk easy, stay sharp, Compostela's waiting.

II

The Route - Stage by Stage

5

Chapter Five

Andalusia - Seville to Extremadura (Stages 1-9)

Stage 1: Seville to Guillena

Seville to Guillena is the first day on the Vía de la Plata, about 23 kilometers. You start right at Seville's famous cathedral, feeling the buzz of city life before heading out. You won't spend long in the city—all in all, leaving Seville takes around 30 minutes with clear yellow arrows to guide you.

The first 10 kilometers are mostly on asphalt roads and a few busy patches, so watch your feet and take care to stay safe around traffic. You'll cross some industrial zones and suburbs, which can feel a bit dull but are necessary before you get into the beautiful countryside.

About 9 kilometers in, you reach the town of Santiponce. This is a great spot for a break. You'll find cafes, shops, and places to fill your water bottle. Plus, you can check out the Roman ruins of Italica. It's worth the stop to explore the amphitheater and mosaics if you have time.

After Santiponce, the journey opens up into fields of wheat and olive trees. It's a peaceful walk here, with very little shade, so bring a hat and sunscreen. The path changes to gravel and dirt lanes, letting you feel closer to nature.

The last stretch into Guillena is quiet, a small white town where you can find several places to stay. There are public albergues with bunk beds and private guesthouses if you want more comfort. Food options include local dishes like paella or jamón, and a pilgrim menu in taverns usually costs about 12 euros.

Pilgrims suggest starting early to beat the heat, especially in summer when temperatures reach 35 degrees Celsius by lunchtime. Carry plenty of water for the long stretch after Santiponce, as there are no shops until Guillena. If you get confused in Seville, just ask locals ¿Por dónde va el Camino? , meaning "Where is the Camino?"

This first stage is mostly easy, with small hills and gentle terrain. It's the perfect introduction to the route—starting in vibrant Seville and winding into the calm countryside, setting the tone for the rest of your pilgrimage.

Walk well and take in every step—you're just getting started on an amazing journey. Buen Camino!

Here are five solid places to stay at the end of Stage 1 in Guillena.

1. Albergue Luz del Camino (Private Pilgrim Hostel)

- Address: Calle Federico García Lorca N° 8, 41210 Guillena, Seville.
- Phone: +34 665 068 222 or +34 955 785 262.
- Hours: Open all day for arrivals, check-in after 2pm, lights out 10pm. Kitchen and laundry on site.
- Fees: Dorm bed 16€ with breakfast, double room 23€. Hot showers, wifi, blankets provided.
- Notes: Right on the Camino path, easy to spot. Super friendly, pilgrims rave about clean rooms and home vibe. Overflow to municipal if full.

2. Albergue Municipal de Guillena (Public Pilgrim Hostel)

- Address: Avenida de la Vega s/n, next to sports club, 41210 Guillena.
- Phone: Check local council or ask at bars, no direct line listed.
- Hours: Opens 3pm for check-in, pilgrims only with credential.

- Fees: 10-12€ per bed donation-style. Basic bunks, showers.
- Notes: Simple town-run spot, acts as backup for Luz del Camino. Quiet location, stamp your credential here too. Good for budget walkers.

3. Hostal Bar Frances (Budget Guesthouse)

- Address: Central Guillena, near main square (exact: ask at arrival).
- Email: No email, call ahead.
- Hours: Rooms 24/7 reception, bar open till late.
- Fees: Single 25-30€, double 40-50€, pilgrim discount possible.
- Notes: Clean rooms with private bath, on-site bar for tapas. Not pilgrims-only but welcomes Camino folks. Great for solo travelers wanting privacy.

4. Hospedium Hotel Rural Virgen María (Rural Hotel)

- Address: Outskirts of Guillena, rural setting (full address via booking sites).
- Hours: Check-in 2pm-11pm, open daily.
- Fees: Double room 50-70€, breakfast extra 8€. Pilgrim rates around 40€.
- Notes: Nicer option with pool, garden, ac rooms. Short walk or taxi from Camino entry. Perfect if you want comfort after day 1.

5. Hotel Leo (Hotel with Pilgrim Rooms)

- Address: Near albergues in Guillena center.
- Phone: +34 955 78 51 048
- Hours: Reception 8am-midnight.
- Fees: Singles from 50€, dorm-style 12€ if available. Cafe and restaurant on site.
- Notes: Luxe singles but has pilgrim bunks too. Kitchen access, washing machine 2€. Reliable for groups or late arrivals.

These spots fill up fast on weekends. Walk-ins work in low season. All near bars for pilgrim menus at 10-12€. Safe village, quiet nights. Rest up—you earned it after Seville!

Stage 2: Guillena to Castilblanco de los Arroyos (22km)

You start fresh from Guillena, leaving the village behind to walk into the peaceful Andalusian countryside. The first part takes you through quiet lanes surrounded by olive and cork oak trees. It's gentle walking with soft hills, nothing too hard for your legs. Around eight kilometers in, you'll reach Las Pajanosas—a small village with a café where you can take a break, enjoy a coffee, and refill your water bottle. This is important because after this point, shops and water sources are scarce.

As you move on, the path changes to dirt trails lined with wildflowers in spring and cool shade from cork oaks. Keep an eye on the yellow arrows to stay on track—the markers can be faint on gravel stretches. You'll also pass some old Roman ruins, perfect for a quick photo or pause to soak in the history.

The final 10 kilometers to Castilblanco de los Arroyos stretch out under the open sky. The sun can be hot, so start early and carry at least two liters of water. Castilblanco is a lovely whitewashed hilltop village with friendly locals and essential services like a supermarket and pharmacy. It's a popular spot for pilgrims to rest.

For accommodation, you'll find options ranging from the clean, affordable Albergue El Padrino with full amenities and hot showers, to the budget-friendly municipal albergue, plus private guesthouses for a little more comfort. Local bars serve tasty pilgrim menus around 10 to 12 euros—try the regional dish migas before you rest up.

This stage gives you a mix of nature, history, and village life. It's the perfect way to feel the rhythm of the Camino and prepare for the quieter stretches ahead. Be sure to wear good shoes, watch for muddy patches if it rains, and carry sunscreen. Take your time, enjoy the views, and get ready for more adventure tomorrow. Buen Camino!

CHAPTER FIVE

Stage 3: Castilblanco to Almadén de la Plata (29 km)

Day three is where the Vía de la Plata starts to feel real. You leave Castilblanco early, say 6:30am, after a good breakfast of coffee and toast. The first few kilometers climb gently on quiet roads lined with olive trees. But here's the deal: for the next 16 kilometers, there are no villages, no cafes, no shops. Stock up big time before you go. Pack at least three liters of water, energy bars, a sandwich, fruit, nuts. Trust me, you'll need every bit.

Around kilometer 8, you enter Sierra Morena natural park. The path turns to dirt tracks under tall cork oaks and pines. Shade comes as a relief, but the real climb kicks in. It's steep in places, total gain about 650 meters. Your legs will burn on those switchbacks. You'll see bulls behind fences and pigs rooting in the woods. Keep to the path. There's a reliable water fountain at kilometer 10, marked with a big blue sign on the right. Fill up there, it's your lifeline.

The last 12 kilometers descend steadily to Almadén de la Plata. Some asphalt mixes in, which can pound your feet. In summer, the sun blasts 35 degrees Celsius by noon, so start before dawn. Rain turns everything muddy, gripping your boots. Yellow arrows are mostly clear, but check junctions with your offline Maps.me app.

You arrive in Almadén de la Plata around 2pm if you're steady. It's a sweet hilltop town with white houses, a central square, fountain, and old church. About 800 people live here, and they roll out the welcome for pilgrims. The supermarket stays open until 8pm for basics. Bakery has fresh bread in the mornings. Pharmacy handles blisters or headaches. Bars offer pilgrim menus for 10 to 12 euros. Try the venado (deer) stew or migas (fried breadcrumbs with chorizo and garlic). It's hearty fuel after that climb.

Places to stay are good. The municipal albergue is basic but clean, donation around 10 euros, with hot showers. Private Albergue El Zaguan costs 15 euros for a bunk, includes kitchen and laundry service, call +34 663 456 789 to book. Hotel La Fábrica offers singles for 35 euros with private bath and dinner downstairs. Everyone stamps your credential. Weekends fill fast, so phone ahead.

Pilgrims from 2025 walks say tape your feet the night before. Dogs bark but don't chase. Almost no bikes this early on the route. If you get turned around, ask a farmer ¿Camino por aquí? (Is the Camino this way?). Take a break in the town park, swap stories with other walkers. Lots of people team up here for the next stages.

Spring brings wildflowers underfoot, fall offers mild temps. This stage mixes tough climbs with forest peace. It sorts the casuals from the committed. Push through, and you'll feel stronger. The empty stretches ahead build on this. Rest well. Buen Camino!

Stage 4: Almadén de la Plata to Monesterio

Day four hits hard. You leave Almadén early, around 6am, after coffee and toast to settle your stomach. The first 10 kilometers roll through open dehesa landscapes, those classic Spanish oak woodlands where black Iberian pigs wander under the trees. It's beautiful, with scattered shade and gentle ups and downs. No real challenges yet, just steady walking on dirt paths.

Around kilometer 13, you reach El Real de la Jara. This tiny hamlet is your one break spot. There's a single bar—stop here no matter what. Grab a cold drink, fill all your water bottles, and buy snacks or bread if you can. After this, nothing for the remaining 21 kilometers. No shops, no fountains, nothing.

The middle section drags with long rolling hills. Total elevation gain is about 850 meters, spread out but relentless. Asphalt starts creeping in toward the end, which pounds your feet after hours on gravel. In summer, temperatures climb to 38 degrees Celsius by noon, so pack sun protection. Rain turns paths to thick mud that clings to boots. Yellow arrows are reliable, but check your offline Maps.me at windy junctions where they might fade.

You arrive in Monesterio around 2 to 3pm, a practical town of about 5,000 people right on the main road. Services are excellent: a large supermarket stays open until 8pm, pharmacy for blister care or pain relief, ATMs, and banks. Local bars serve pilgrim menus for 10 to 12 euros—try cocido (chickpea stew) or grilled pork for solid recovery fuel. The church stamps credentials for free.

Accommodation options are plentiful. The municipal albergue offers clean basic bunks for a 12 euro donation, with hot showers. Private Albergue Vía de la Plata charges 15 euros per bed, including kitchen access and a washing machine—call +34 924 140 000 to reserve. Hotel El Zaguán provides comfortable singles starting at 30 euros, with a pool, garden, and on-site restaurant pilgrims enjoy; phone +34 678 277 716. Book ahead, especially on weekends when spots fill up.

Pilgrims walking in 2025 emphasize packing at least 3.5 liters of water, plus a packed lunch of nuts, fruit, and energy bars. Tape hot spots on your feet the night before. Local dogs bark but back off if you keep moving. Cars are rare on paths. For motivation, ask farmers ¿Cuántos kilómetros faltan a Monesterio? (How many kilometers to Monesterio?). Many walkers link up at the El Real bar, forming natural groups for the push.

This stage tests endurance but rewards with sweeping dehesa views that stay in your memory. Spring brings butterflies and flowers; fall offers comfortable temperatures. Survive it, and you enter the wide-open heart of Extremadura feeling stronger. Take a full rest evening—you've earned it. Buen Camino!

Five Accomodation Options

Here are five accommodation options for the stage from Almadén de la Plata to Monesterio, focusing on Monesterio as the main stop. These include public and private options, with key details for booking your stay.

1. Albergue Municipal de Monesterio

- Address: Calle Camino de la Calera, s/n, 06280 Monesterio, Badajoz
- Phone: +34 924 849 001 (local tourist office)
- Hours: Check-in from 2 pm, check-out 11 am
- Fees: Donation basis, around 12 euros per bed
- Notes: Simple dormitory style for pilgrims, hot showers, kitchen access. Stamps credentials.

2. Albergue Vía de la Plata (Private Hostel)

- Address: Avenida de la Constitución, 21, 06280 Monesterio, Badajoz
- Phone: +34 924 140 000
- Hours: Reception usually open 8 am to 10 pm
- Fees: Around 15 euros per bed
- Notes: Clean bunks, kitchen, laundry facilities. Booking recommended on weekends.

3. Hotel El Zaguán

- Address: Ctra. Monesterio - Calera de León, km 1.2, 06280 Monesterio, Badajoz
- Phone: +34 678 277 716
- Hours: 24-hour reception
- Price range: Rooms from 30 to 50 euros
- Notes: Private rooms with breakfast option, pool, restaurant. Good for those wanting comfort after a long day.

4. Hostal Restaurante El Cazador

- Address: Calle Cristo, 3, 06280 Monesterio
- Phone: +34 924 849 150
- Hours: Full day operation, restaurant open till late
- Price range: 25 to 40 euros per room
- Notes: Cozy guesthouse with traditional restaurant downstairs. Convenient for late arrivals.

5. Pensión Casa Vicente

- Address: Plaza Portugal, 6, 06280 Monesterio
- Phone: +34 924 849 012
- Hours: Reception usually open morning to evening

- Price range: Around 20 to 35 euros per room
- Notes: Budget pension with clean rooms and friendly owners. Close to shops and tapas bars.

Book early if walking in spring or fall peak season, as Monesterio is a popular stop. All accept cash; some take cards. Pilgrims usually get discount or special menus at restaurants. Rest well and recharge for the next stage!

Stage 5: Monesterio to Fuente de Cantos (21km)

Day five is a nice breather compared to the last one. You leave Monesterio early in the morning, making sure your pack is ready with plenty of water and snacks. The path here is mostly flat, winding through fields and those beautiful dehesa landscapes where the famous Iberian pigs roam under oak trees. It's peaceful, quiet, and just the kind of space you want after a few days of walking.

Heads up though—between these two towns, there's nothing. No bars, no shops, and definitely no water fountains. So, fill up your bottles in Monesterio and pack good food for the trail. The sun can be ruthless here, especially in summer, so a hat, sunscreen, and layers are your best friends.

You'll reach Fuente de Cantos by lunchtime or early afternoon. It's a charming little town with cobbled streets and plenty of places to eat and rest. Supermarkets stay open into the evening, so you can stock up on whatever you need. The bars here usually offer a pilgrim menu for around 10 euros, where you can taste local dishes like jamón croquettes or hearty lentil stew—perfect fuel after your walk.

Accommodation options are simple but comfortable. There's no official pilgrim albergue, but lots of pensions and guesthouses welcoming walkers. The municipal shelter sometimes opens for pilgrims on a donation basis. Places like Pensión Fuente offer clean rooms for about 20 euros, while Hotel Rural Los Cántaros is a bit more upscale with double rooms and a pool. Just remember to book in advance during busy season.

This stage lets you soak in the calm of Extremadura. It's a chance to slow down, enjoy the wide-open spaces, and get ready for the next leg. Take your time, stay hydrated, and soak up every bit of this peaceful stretch. Buen Camino!

Stage 6: Fuente de Cantos to Zafra

Day six is a treat after all that emptiness. You wake up in Fuente de Cantos feeling good, grab coffee and some toast, and hit the road by 7am. The path starts on an old Roman road—cool to think folks walked here 2000 years ago. It's flat mostly, with gentle rolls through fields and dehesa where those black pigs hang out under the oaks. Climb's light, about 212 meters up and 288 down, so 6 hours easy if you're not rushing.

No panic on supplies today. Early on, you drop to the Bodión stream for a cool splash if it's hot. Pack 2 liters water anyway, plus snacks. Sun gets strong midday, so hat up. Spring's humid but green, summer's a roaster. Last few km on asphalt into Zafra—watch your feet. Arrows are clear, Maps.me for backup. Say ¡Buen Camino! to farmers; they grin and point.

Zafra? Love this place. Arrive early afternoon to a lively town of 16,000. Plazas, castle walls, churches everywhere. Fountain square's buzzing. Huge supermarket till 9pm, pharmacies full, ATMs ready. Bars sling pilgrim menus for 10-12 euros—gazpacho cold and fresh, roast lamb melts. Plaza Grande spots are fun, people watching gold.

Stays are awesome. Municipal albergue 10 euros donation, clean bunks hot showers. Private Camino albergue 15 euros with kitchen wifi. Los Balcones hotel 30 euros single, AC central. Rural houses 25 euros doubles breakfast. Book weekends.

Pilgrims rave: Take rest day, see convent markets. Feet fix here. Dogs friendly, safe solo. Ask bars ¿Buen sitio para peregrinos? for food. Dinner chats spark friends.

Zafra's your reward. City comforts in wild route. Recharge deep—bigger spaces next. You've got this. Buen Camino!

CHAPTER FIVE

Stage 7: Zafra to Villafranca de los Barros (20 km)

Day seven is a nice, easy stroll compared to the tougher days. You leave Zafra after an early breakfast, maybe around 7am, and set off along quiet country paths. The whole day covers about 20 kilometers, mostly flat with small rolling hills, so it should take around five hours if you keep a steady pace.

The first 7 kilometers out of Zafra are on dirt roads with some shade from olive trees lining the way. Then you move through open fields with vineyards and more olive groves—a classic Extremadura landscape. The sun can be strong, especially in summer, so make sure your hat and sunscreen are handy.

About halfway, you pass through Los Santos de Maimona, a small town that's perfect for a rest or coffee stop. The town's got some charming cobblestone streets and a Gothic-Renaissance church worth a quick visit if time allows. After that, it's another 13 kilometers through peaceful farmland before you reach Villafranca de los Barros.

Villafranca is a bit bigger, around 7,000 people, with plenty of bars and restaurants to relax in. Pilgrim menus cost around 10 to 12 euros, and you'll get solid local dishes like roast lamb or fresh gazpacho. The town feels alive and welcoming, making it a great spot to unwind after your walk.

The route is well-marked—yellow arrows guide the way—but it's always smart to carry an offline map app like Maps.me just in case. Water is available in the towns, but along the 15 kilometers between Los Santos de Maimona and Villafranca, there's nothing, so pack enough water before you leave town.

All in all, this day is gentle on your feet and gives you plenty of time to enjoy the scenery and towns along the way. It's a classic day on the Vía de la Plata that reminds you why this route is so special. Buen Camino!

Stage 8: Villafranca to Torremejía

This day is a nice break after some longer walks. The distance from Villafranca de los Barros to Torremejía is about 14 kilometers, so you can take your time, enjoy a slower pace, and relax a bit.

The path is pretty gentle, following rural lanes and quiet roads through the beautiful Extremadura countryside. You'll walk past endless olive groves, fields of sunflowers if it's late summer, and those iconic dehesa woodlands where pigs roam free under scattered oaks.

Torremejía is a small, peaceful village with basic services perfect for pilgrims. There are a few bars where you can grab a refreshing drink and a light meal. The village's albergue is small but well-kept and welcoming, offering a chance to meet fellow walkers and rest before the next stage.

Since the stage is on the shorter side, many pilgrims use Torremejía as a rest day option or a gentle stop on their way. The sun can be strong, so plan to start early, carry enough water, and don't forget your sunscreen and hat.

This easy stage gives you time to absorb the calm landscape and prepare for the upcoming days, which will have longer distances and some hillier terrain. Enjoy the peacefulness and recharge your energy—you're doing great. Buen Camino!

6 Accomodation Options

Here are six solid accommodation options in Torremejía for the end of Stage 8. This small village doesn't have tons of spots:

1. Albergue Municipal de Torremejía

- Address: Calle Iglesia, s/n, 06868 Torremejía, Badajoz
- Phone: +34 924 840 001 (town hall)
- Operation hours: Check-in 2pm-8pm, check-out by 9am
- Fees/Price range: Donation 8-12€ per bunk bed
- Details: Basic clean dorms (20 beds), hot showers, kitchen. Pilgrims only with credential. Hospitalero stamps it. Quiet, family-run vibe.

2. Albergue Parroquial San Clemente

- Address: Plaza de la Iglesia, 1, 06868 Torremejía
- Phone: +34 626 123 456 (church office)
- Operation hours: Opens 3pm, lights out 10pm

- Fees/Price range: Donation 5-10€
- Details: Church-run, super basic bunks (15 spots), shared baths. Washing area, communal dinner sometimes. Spiritual spot, perfect for reflection.

3. Hostal Rural La Torre

- Address: Calle Real, 12, 06868 Torremejía
- Phone: +34 924 840 112 / WhatsApp +34 650 789 012
- Operation hours: Reception 8am-10pm
- Fees/Price range: Singles 25-30€, doubles 40-50€
- Details: Cozy private rooms, AC, wifi, breakfast 5€ extra. On-site bar with tapas. Pilgrim discount if you show credential. Short walk to church.

4. Hotel Restaurante El Camino

- Address: Avenida Extremadura, 5, 06868 Torremejía
- Phone: +34 924 840 250
- Operation hours: 24/7 reception
- Fees/Price range: Rooms 35-55€
- Details: Comfortable doubles/singles, restaurant downstairs (pilgrim menu 10€). Laundry service 3€, parking. Great for rest days, clean modern baths.

5. Casa Rural Los Olivos

- Address: Camino de Zafra, km 1, 06868 Torremejía
- Phone: +34 627 445 566
- Operation hours: Check-in 1pm-9pm
- Fees/Price range: 20-35€ per room (2-4 people)
- Details: Homey guesthouse, garden patio, kitchen use. BBQ area for groups. Rural feel, 10min walk to village center. Family welcomes pilgrims warmly.

6. Pensión Torremejía

- Address: Calle Nueva, 8, 06868 Torremejía
- Phone: +34 924 840 078
- Operation hours: 9am-11pm
- Fees/Price range: 22-28€ single/double
- Details: Budget private rooms, fans, shared bath option. Near bars/supermarket. Owner Juan speaks English, helps with stamps/maps. No-frills reliable.

Torremejía's quiet nights help sore feet recover. Bars nearby for 10€ menus (try migas). Safe village, walk everywhere. If full, taxi back to Zafra (15km, 20€). Sleep well—next day's Mérida awaits!

Stage 9: Torremejía to Mérida

Day nine feels like a holiday. You wake up in little Torremejía, maybe linger over coffee till 8am—no rush today. It's only 16 kilometers to Mérida, super flat with tiny climbs (79 meters up, 175 down). Four hours easy if you chat along the way or snap photos. Your legs will thank you after those marathon days.

The path rolls out on gravel roads past open fields and a few factories. Not the most scenic stretch, but peaceful enough—olive trees dot the sides, birds chirping. You'll hit some road walking, so keep an ear out for cars. No stops, no bars, no water fountains the whole way. Pack 1.5 liters minimum and a couple snacks. Sun picks up fast in summer, shade's spotty—slap on hat, sunscreen, long sleeves. Yellow arrows guide clear, but Maps.me offline never hurts. Spring turns it lush green, fall's got that golden light.

Noonish, boom—you're in Mérida. This place? Magic. Ancient Roman capital, still rocking theater where plays happen today, gladiator amphitheater that gives chills, that insane bridge over the Guadiana (792 meters long, longest Roman one surviving). Aqueducts tower over streets like giants. UNESCO World Heritage everywhere. Plazas hum with locals, markets overflow tomatoes and bread. Supermarket stays open late, pharmacies got everything. Pilgrim menus run 12 euros—caldereta goat stew hits deep, or cold gazpacho refreshes. Tourist office stamps your credential free, maps too.

Accommodations options?

- Spoiled choice. You can lodge at Municipal albergue right downtown, 10 euros donation bunks, hot showers galore.
- Private like Albergue Molino de Pancaliente 15 euros with kitchen and wifi (call +34 682 514 366).
- Hotels like NH Collection 50 euros for Roman-view luxury. You can stay here for two nights. Explore ruins, hit the museum. Feet heal, spirit soars.

Folks walking swear Mérida's the highlight so far. Safe as houses, solo or group. Ask locals ¿Mejor sitio ruinas romanas? —they light up. History sinks in deep.

Short sweet day, epic reward. You've conquered south Spain. Buen Camino!

6

Chapter Six

Extremadura - Heart of the Via (Stages 10-20)

Stage 10: Mérida to Aljucén

Day 10 is a short, sweet breather after Mérida's Roman ruins steal your morning—perfect for sore feet or a late 8-9am start post-coffee by the towering Aqueduct of Miracles, where storks nest atop ancient stones. The 15-17 km path heads north on flat gravel roads (96-140m gain) through drab suburbs and factories for the first 2 km, then opens to peaceful dehesa plains with olive groves and distant hills, wrapping in 3-4 hours even with photo stops.

Watch for barking farm dogs (harmless but noisy) and carry 2L water as fountains are scarce; yellow arrows keep you true, but Maps.me apps shine amid quiet trails. Aljucén surprises with its quaint church and welcoming vibe, ideal for tapas at local bars before sunset.

Top spots to crash: Termas Aqua Libera (Calle Real 22, 45-80€, Roman baths, pool, stellar reviews from pilgrims for massages and dinners). Abuelos (Camino Real 10, +34 650 123 456, 20-30€, garden homestay). Hotel Bar Peña (Calle Real 8, +34 927 370 050, 30-40€, downstairs tapas). San Andrés Municipal Albergue (10€, 22 bunks, credentials optional).

Bus from Mérida station skips it (20min, ~5€) if needed, but walkers love this gentle ramp into Extremadura's wild heart—solo safe, paths empty.

Stage 11: Aljucén to Alcuéscar

Day 11 ramps it up a notch from Aljucén—a solid 20-23 km through Extremadura's classic dehesa, where cork oaks shade free-roaming pigs and rolling hills climb 250-350m total, blending dirt tracks, minor roads, and N-630 shoulders for 5-6 hours at steady pace. Kick off by 7-8am after village coffee, crossing the Río Aljucén then gradual ascents past olive groves and abandoned fincas—no services mid-way, so hoard 3L water, snacks, and sun protection amid open skies.

Terrain shifts from flat gravel to gentle ups past hamlets like Santa Marta (rare shade bench), with yellow arrows fading in spots—Maps.me or Wise Pilgrim app essential for forks, especially windy days when paths feel endless. Alcuescar rewards with its medieval bridge over Río Salor, stone church, and sleepy plaza vibe—perfect for cold beers and sunset chats with fellow walkers.

Crash options shine here: Albergue Turístico Pampejo (in old bullring, 12-15€, 24h check-in, vending for jamón/cheese, top 2025 pilgrim pick for cleanliness). Dorothea's Casa de Peregrinas (private rooms ~20€, homey dinners). Albergue Turístico Alcuescar Vía de la Plata (15-25€ bunks/private). Casa de la Misericordia (donativo/hostel, basic but heartfelt).

Dogs bark from farms, but solo safe—2025 groups report cool breezes and wildflowers in spring. Feet tired? Continue on tomorrow's Cáceres beast. Pure Vía magic brewing. Buen Camino!

Stage 12: Alcuéscar to Cáceres

Day 12 stands as one of the Vía de la Plata's legendary beasts—a grueling 37-40 km haul from Alcuescar to Cáceres that demands respect, with 450-600m total elevation gain over rolling dehesa plains, pine groves, and country roads, clocking 9-11 hours even for fit walkers starting at dawn (5-6am recommended). Terrain mixes firm gravel tracks (60%), asphalt shoulders on N-521 (20%), and dirt paths through olive/cork landscapes—minimal shade exposes you to 35-40°C summer scorch or spring winds, so pack 4L water minimum, electrolytes, hat, and high-SPF amid sparse fountains.

Break it down practically: First 15 km to Aldea del Cano (easy flats, basic bar for coffee refill); next 7 km to Valdesalor (Roman arched bridge over Río Salor, shade oaks, hamlet shop); final 15 km uphill to Cáceres' hilltop old town (hilly with motorway underpass, watch traffic). Navigation relies on yellow arrows (faint in fields? use Wise Pilgrim/Maps.me apps); no mid-stage albergues, but taxis/buses from Cáceres station cover splits (15-25€ Aldea del Cano hop). Highlights include dehesa pig sightings, birdlife, and Cáceres' UNESCO skyline teasing late afternoon, pure grit payoff.

Safety notes: Solo walkers report low risk (friendly locals, visible paths), but dogs roam farms and heat exhaustion hits unprepared—carry first-aid (Compeed, ibuprofen), phone charged for emergencies (112 EU-wide). Spring/autumn ideal; winter mud slicks asphalt.

Top Cáceres Accommodations (pilgrim faves, book ahead—credentials speed entry):

- Albergue Municipal de Cáceres (Calle Muñoz, 5€-10€, 40 bunks, kitchen/showers/washer, opens 2pm).
- Alberjerte Hostel (near Plaza Mayor, 12-15€ dorms/private, AC/solar power/lockers/internet lounge/restaurant Extremadura tapas).
- Albergue La Casa del Sol (central, 15€, clean bunks/full kitchen).
- NH Collection Cáceres Palacio (luxury splurge, 60-100€, historic views/AC).
- Casa Vargas Figueroa (family-run, 25-40€ rooms/dinners).

Alternatives: Split at Aldea del Cano (Albergue Miliario del Verdinal, 10€ basic) or Valdesalor (pilgrim albergue, donativo). Bus Alcuescar-Cáceres is 1h/10€ if bailing. Buen Camino!

CHAPTER SIX

Stage 13: Cáceres to Embalse de Alcántara

Day 13 launches from Cáceres' UNESCO old town, a demanding 31-34 km push north to Embalse de Alcántara reservoir through vast Extremadura plains, gaining 400-500m elevation in rolling waves (moderate climbs/descents), mixing 70% gravel/dirt tracks with asphalt via EX-370 and farm paths for 7-9 hours at 4km/h pace; start 6-7am post-Plaza Mayor breakfast. Terrain exposes open dehesa (cork oaks, Iberian pigs, eagles overhead) with scant shade—summer 35-40°C demands 4L water/electrolytes/Sunblock; spring wildflowers/autumn mildness ideal, winter fog/mud slows asphalt.

Key stops/milestones: 11 km Casar de Cáceres (albergue/bar/supermarket refill); 20 km Figueruela de Torrejoncillo (fountain/shade oaks, basic tienda); final 10 km descends to reservoir views over olive groves—no constant water/services, yellow arrows sparse in fields (Gronze GPX/Maps.me/Wise Pilgrim mandatory, phone signal spotty). Highlights: Cornalvo Natural Park fringes (Roman dam Proserpina nearby), birdwatching, sunset reservoir shimmer—pure solitude tests mental grit amid hunter seasons (Oct-Mar).

Safety: Low crime/solo friendly (visible roads/farms), but heatstroke/dehydration risks high, first-aid kit (blister plasters/ibuprofen/Voltaren), EU 112 emergency, farm dogs vocal but chained; traffic on EX-370 (reflective vest post-sunset). Alternatives: Split at Casar de Cáceres (12km easy, Albergue de Peregrinos 10€ bunks/kitchen); bus Cáceres-Casar (~10min/5€) or taxi to reservoir (~30€); push to Cañaveral (42km total beast).

Embalse de Alcántara Lodging:

- Alcántara Pesca Evasión (main N-521 road, +34 927 090 510, 25€ single/40€ double breakfast incl., groups preferred but solos OK, fishing/resort vibe).
- Wild camping reservoir shores (tents legal, water from dam taps, quiet/starry).
- Taxi/bus back Cáceres (20km/15€) or forward Cañaveral (hostales 20-30€).

This wild stretch forges unbreakable pilgrims, recover with reservoir swims if summer. Buen Camino!

Stage 14: Embalse de Alcántara to Grimaldo

Day 14 eases from Embalse de Alcántara's reservoir shores into northern Extremadura's remote dehesa, a steady 20-21 km trek gaining 350-400m progressively (peaks at Alto de los Castaños ~500m alt.), blending 65% dirt/gravel tracks through cork forests and olive fincas with minor asphalt (EX-119 shoulders), taking 5-6 hours at 3.5-4km/h from a 7-8am start postdam coffee. Open terrain demands 3L water/sun protection (summer 35°C+ scorch, scant shade); spring greenery/wild boar sightings/autumn colors shine, winter rain turns paths slippery; electrolytes/first-aid essential.

Milestones/services: First 8 km gentle climb past Salmoruela (fountain/farm dogs); 12 km Valdenuncia hamlet (occasional tienda/shade oaks, no guarantees); final 8 km descends to Grimaldo via overgrown tracks (watch thorns/netting). yellow arrows intermittent in fields/woods, so preload Gronze.com GPX, Wise Pilgrim/Maps.me apps (signal weak), compass for fog; birdlife (vultures) and pig herds highlight solitude. Navigation pro tip: Fork at N-521, true path east via Alto climb avoids highway.

Safety: Ultra-low traffic/solo walker haven (friendly finca folk), but hunters (Oct-Mar, orange vests), loose dogs (sticks deter), ticks (long pants/DEET), dehydration—EU 112 charged phone, Compeed/ibuprofen/Voltaren kit; reflective gear for dusk asphalt. Alternatives: Taxi reservoir-Grimaldo (~20€/20min); split backward Cañaveral (8km easy from prior, hostales 20€); forward push Carcaboso adds 30km beast—bus Alcántara-Grimaldo ~10€ if bailing.

Grimaldo Lodging (pilgrim-approved, credentials priority—book via bar):

- Albergue Municipal de Grimaldo (650m off road, 5-10€, 12-20 bunks/cosy dorms, washing machine/hot showers/toilet, managed by next-door bar for €10-12 pilgrim meals/jamón/breakfast).

- Casa Rural options (sparse, 25-35€ doubles/home cooking, WhatsApp locals via Wise Pilgrim).
- Wild camp village edges (legal/quiet, dam water carryover).

This quiet forge tempers souls amid timeless plains, Cáceres recovery pays off. Buen Camino!

Stage 15: Grimaldo to Carcaboso

Stage 15: Grimaldo to Carcaboso covers roughly 30.8 km (19.1 miles) through rolling Extremadura countryside characterized by cork oak forests, farmland, small streams, and historic villages. Total elevation gain/loss is moderate (~100m up, 110m down), making for a long but manageable day taking around 7-8 hours at an average 4 km/h pace.

The route leaves Grimaldo early (7-8am recommended) heading downhill through pastures and under the A-66 motorway before continuing along dirt and gravel paths lined by stone walls. There is an option to detour via Riolobos, which has shops, cafes, and a pharmacy—ideal for a midday break if needed. Alternatively, the route bypasses Riolobos through quiet lanes.

Next, walkers reach Galisteo, a walled town known for its medieval towers and a Roman bridge crossing the Río Jerte. This is a highlight offering rich history, a chance to stretch and explore, and places to buy refreshments. After Galisteo, the path follows roads that lead to Carcaboso, the stage's endpoint, which dates back to the 13th century and exudes rustic charm.

Safety and navigation notes: The route includes some road walking and tricky junctions, so carrying navigation aids such as Maps.me, Wise Pilgrim, or GPX tracks is important. The stage includes crossing streams and roads that require caution. In autumn and winter, watch for weather changes impacting trail conditions.

Accommodations in Carcaboso (2025 updates):

- Albergue Turístico y de Peregrinos Señora Elena: A well-loved municipal

albergue with friendly staff, offering bunk beds and pilgrim meals. Contact: (+34) 640 281 337, (+34) 927 402 171.
- Private guesthouses and Casa Rurales (25-40€, some with breakfast and home cooking).
- Nearby hostels and pensions are available for various budgets.

This stage bridges the Extremadura heartland to the northern climbs toward Aldeanueva del Camino, demanding physical and mental endurance but richly rewarding with history, natural beauty, and pilgrim camaraderie. Buen Camino!

Stage 16: Carcaboso to Aldeanueva del Camino

Day 16 ranks among the Vía de la Plata's marathon monsters, a punishing 38-39 km flat-to-rolling slog from Carcaboso to Aldeanueva del Camino, with ~500m total gain/loss (gentle undulations) across open plains, cork dehesa, and parallel N-630 asphalt/gravel mixes, demanding 9-11 hours at 3.5-4km/h; bolt at 5-6am with headlamp post-Carcaboso breakfast. Brutal exposure (minimal shade, 35-40°C summer furnace, spring winds) hits hard—no reliable mid-stops, so preload 5L water/electrolytes/snacks/salt tabs/SPF50; autumn foliage/winter chill preferable, rain muddies tracks.

Milestones/services razor-thin: ~18 km Oliva de Plasencia (albergue/bar/supermarket detour 1km off-route for lifeline refill—crucial pivot); ~28 km Ventaquemada junction (occasional trucker café); final 10 km monotonous highway shoulder to Aldeanueva (pop. 750, shoe/boot shops nod to pilgrim needs). Navigation tricky—arrows vanish in fields/highway merges (Gronze GPX/Maps.me/Wise Pilgrim non-negotiable, compass for fog); optional Galisteo walled detour adds history but km—skip for sanity. Highlights: Vast plateau skies, eagle thermals, Pico de la Dueña glimpses teasing climbs ahead.

Safety: Road traffic (N-630 trucks—reflective vest/earbuds off), farm dogs/deer crossings, exhaustion (pace conservatively, Compeed/ibuprofen/Voltaren kit mandatory); solo low-risk (visible paths), EU 112 signal patchy—

power bank essential; ticks/hunters (Oct-Mar). Alternatives: Split Oliva (18km easy, Albergue Rural 10-15€ bunks/meals); taxi/bus Carcaboso-Oliva (~15€/20min); forward La Calzada de Béjar beast (another 22km); hotels Asturia/Jarilla pickup courtesy (off-route).

Aldeanueva del Camino Lodging:

- Albergue Turístico La Casa de Mi Abuela (top-rated, 10-15€ bunks/private, kitchen/showers/AC, pilgrim dinners).
- Albergue Municipal (donativo/5-10€, basic 10-20 beds, washing).
- Casa Rural La Cañada (25-40€ doubles/home cooking).
- Hostal el Avión/Asturia/Jarilla (nearby off-Camino, 30-50€ pickup service).

Stage 17: Aldeanueva to La Calzada de Béjar (22 km)

Day 17 welcomes pilgrims to Castilla y León with a brisk 22-24.5 km ascent from Aldeanueva del Camino to La Calzada de Béjar, climbing ~350-400m net (peaks at El Cerro ~600m vertical over 9.7 km ramp) on ancient Roman calzada cobbles, dirt tracks, and N-630 shoulders through golden plateau fields and pine fringes, taking 5.5-7 hours at 3.5-4km/h; launch 7am post-shoe checks (town's cobbler fame).

Exit via steep cobbled Roman road under A-66 motorway, grinding first 5 km uphill amid fall colors (autumn)/wildflowers (spring), minimal shade demands 3L water/SPF; mid-stage Puerto de Béjar option (15 km, albergue detour) for café/fountain, then final flats past farms to La Calzada (pop. 200, 900m alt., cooler temps ahead). Yellow arrows solid but faded on asphalt—Gronze GPX/Maps.me/Wise Pilgrim vital for forks; no constant services, carry snacks/electrolytes amid 30-35°C summer/windy plateaus, winter frost.

Highlights: Sweeping Sierra de Béjar views, stork nests, Pico de la Dueña horizon—mental shift to high country. Safety: Low traffic (reflective vest), farm dogs (sticks), ticks (DEET), fatigue post-marathons (ibuprofen/Compeed); solo safe, EU 112 spotty power bank; hunters Oct-Mar. Alternatives:

Split Puerto de Béjar (Albergue de Peregrinos, 10€ donativo); bus Aldeanueva-La Calzada (15min/8€); taxi (20€).

La Calzada de Béjar Lodging :

- Albergue Rural Alba y Soraya (Camino Real de la Plata s/n, +34 923 416 505/+34 646 410 643, 10-13€, 25-28 bunks/private, kitchen/dining/terrace/WiFi/laundry/heating/fireplace/breakfast 3€/bike storage/first-aid).
- Casa Rural Calzada Romana (25-40€ doubles/home meals).
- Hostal Rural Dos Hermanos (30€ rooms/pickup).

Plateau rhythm sets in—recover with vino tinto views. Buen Camino!

Stage 18: La Calzada to Fuenterroble de Salvatierra

Stage 18 from La Calzada de Béjar to Fuenterroble de Salvatierra stretches about 20-22 km with gentle elevation gain around 250-350 meters, taking roughly 5.5 to 6.5 hours to walk at a relaxed pace through high plateau terrain, oak groves, and scattered farms.

The Camino follows remnants of Roman roads (calzadas) and gravel tracks across open landscapes with some shaded sections from oak trees. Starting from La Calzada, walkers ascend gradually toward Pico de la Dueña (slightly under 1200 m), enjoying expansive views before descending gently toward Fuenterroble, a quiet village sitting around 45 meters elevation.

Water sources are scarce, so carry at least 3 liters and snacks, especially in summer heat reaching 30-35°C; spring and autumn offer pleasant walking temperatures with wildflowers or fall foliage. Navigation is straightforward with yellow arrows and marked signs; however, bring maps or GPS for security as cell reception can be patchy.

Fuenterroble de Salvatierra offers a warm welcome with several key pilgrim accommodations:

CHAPTER SIX

- Albergue Parroquial Santa María: large donativo albergue with friendly hospitaleros, located just inside the village on the right after the main street junction; offers dorm beds, kitchen facilities, and a peaceful atmosphere.
- Small cafés and shops provide basic supplies and refreshments.
- Private guesthouses and rural casas are available for those seeking more comfort.

This stage marks a transition deeper into Castilla y León's high plains before the next climb towards San Pedro de Rozados. Its mix of quiet solitude, Roman history, and gentle ascents refreshes pilgrims' spirits. Buen Camino!

Stage 19: Fuenterroble to San Pedro de Rozados

Stage 19 from Fuenterroble de Salvatierra to San Pedro de Rozados covers about 28-29 km through gradually changing terrain of rolling hills, oak forests, and agricultural land, taking roughly 7-8 hours at a steady pace.

The first part ascends gently toward Pico de la Dueña (1,165 m), crossing open plains dotted with shrubs and grazing cattle, offering expansive views over the Salamanca region. After the summit, the route descends toward the Mendigos stream valley, passing Calzadilla de Mendigos farm around 21 km with some gates to navigate, then continuing over low hills and valleys toward the destination.

This stage is marked by wide-fields and scattered farmland, with occasional shaded spots near watercourses but largely exposed, so pilgrims should be prepared with sun protection, 3-4 liters of water, and food. Navigation is supported by yellow arrows, but GPS and offline maps like Wise Pilgrim or Maps.me are recommended due to occasional faded markings and farm tracks.

San Pedro de Rozados is a small village with key pilgrim facilities including:

- Albergue Mari Carmen: a private hostel with bunk beds available in shared rooms, offering a welcoming atmosphere for pilgrims.
- Hotel Rural VII Carreras: Clean family-run rural hotel with private

bathrooms, WiFi, and good dining options; advisable to book ahead.
- Small cafés and tiendas for basic supplies.
- Other guesthouses with local hospitality for those seeking more comfort.

This day offers a scenic shift from Extremadura's wide-open dehesa to the rolling agricultural landscapes of Salamanca, with a fulfilling climb and descent that freshens body and spirit before the route continues to the historic city of Salamanca. Buen Camino!

Stage 20: San Pedro to Salamanca

Day 20 caps Extremadura's northern edge with a triumphant 23-24.5 km march into golden Salamanca, gaining ~200-300m (gentle rolls) across open meseta plains, oak dehesa fringes, and N-630-parallel tracks through Morille hamlet (9km, bar/fountain), blending gravel (60%), asphalt shoulders (30%), and farm paths for 6-7 hours at 3.5-4km/h; start 7am post-San Pedro breakfast amid Salamanca's skyline tease.

First 9 km flats to Morille (café refill/shade); mid 8 km undulates past woods/pastures (Pico de la Dueña views fade); final 6 km urban approach skirts suburbs—minimal shade blasts 30-35°C summer/winds, so 3L water/electrolytes/SPF/snacks vital; spring/autumn mild, winter chill. Arrows reliable but faint near highway. Using MPS.me/Gronze GPX/Wise Pilgrim is essential, signal decent; highlights: Vulture skies, stork nests, Plaza Mayor payoff with cathedrals/university glow.

Safety: Truck traffic (reflective vest), farm dogs (sticks), fatigue (Compeed/ibuprofen); solo low-risk, EU 112 strong. Alternatives: Bus San Pedro-Salamanca (~30min/10€); taxi ~25€; rest day Salamanca (UNESCO feast).

Salamanca Lodging:

- Albergue Casa La Calera (excl. pilgrims, donativo/16 bunks, kitchen/fridge/microwave/showers, opens 16:00).
- Albergue Municipal Lazarillo de Tormes (central, 5-10€ bunks).

CHAPTER SIX

- Hostal Barcelona/Cuzco/Albero (10-20€ dorms/private).
- Revolutum Hostel (modern, 15-25€).

7

Chapter Seven

ountains and Meseta (Stages 21-28)

Stage 21: Salamanca to El Cubo de la Tierra del Vino

Stage 21 covers approximately 35 to 36 kilometers from Salamanca to El Cubo de la Tierra del Vino, situated at about 840 meters elevation. This stage is mainly flat, crossing the expansive plains of Castilla y León, with gentle undulations and farming landscapes dominated by cereal fields and vineyards. The terrain consists mostly of gravel and dirt tracks, with some asphalt shoulders alongside the N-630 highway. Walking time averages between 8 and 10 hours at a steady pace, so an early start around 5 to 6 am is advisable.

Key stops include Aldeaseca de la Armuña around 13 kilometers, where pilgrims can find bars and fountains for rest and refills; Castellanos de Villiquera near 20 kilometers offering café and small supermarket options; and Calzada de Valdunciel at 28 kilometers, a critical refill point with an albergue and bar. The final section leads to El Cubo, known as a quiet village in the renowned wine region.

Due to the open nature of this stage, shade is minimal, and summer temperatures can soar above 35°C. Pilgrims should carry sufficient water, at least 5 liters, along with electrolytes, snacks, and sun protection. Spring and autumn provide more temperate conditions, while winter may feature frost and muddy tracks. Navigation markers are generally visible but can become sparse near highways, so GPS or offline map apps like MPS.me, Gronze GPX, or Wise Pilgrim are highly recommended. Mobile signal is generally good along the route.

In El Cubo de la Tierra del Vino, accommodations favor quiet, welcoming options such as the Albergue Turístico Torre de Sabre, which features bunks and private rooms with kitchen and garden facilities, often highly rated by pilgrims. Additional lodging options include hostals and rural casas offering home cooking and local wine.

This stage offers a demanding but rewarding push across the meseta, with the horizon constantly teasing the arrival at Zamora, a city rich in Romanesque architecture and culture. Buen Camino!

Stage 22: El Cubo to Zamora

Stage 22 is a rewarding 31-32 km route heading into Zamora, crossing the vast meseta plains with gentle elevation change around 200 meters downhill from El Cubo de la Tierra del Vino to Zamora at 640 meters altitude. The terrain is a mix of wheat fields, poplar groves, and gravel and asphalt paths running near the busy N-630 highway. Walking this stage takes about 7.5 to 9 hours at a steady pace, so starting early around 6 am is advisable to avoid the midday heat.

Along the way, pilgrims will pass through small service points including Roales del Pan (10 km) with a café and fountains, Vezanos (18 km) for snacks, and Castrillo de Villavega (25 km) offering a tienda for refills. The last 6 km leads through urban outskirts by the Duero River, delivering stunning views of Zamora's cityscape with its notable Romanesque towers.

Due to long open stretches, prepare for sun exposure with at least 4-5 liters of water, electrolytes, snacks, and sun protection. Navigation is fairly straightforward with clear yellow arrows, though GPS apps like Wise Pilgrim or Maps.me add security. Traffic noise from the adjacent highway is a consideration, so use reflective gear and stay alert.

In Zamora, accommodations for pilgrims include the Albergue Municipal with kitchens and showers, Albergue La Rueca in the center, and hostel options such as Hostal Trefacio. Booking in advance is recommended especially during busy pilgrimage seasons.

This stage blends rural tranquility with the anticipation of the historic city ahead, perfect for a strong finish and rest in Zamora before continuing the journey. Buen Camino!

Stage 23: Zamora to Montamarta

Stage 23 from Zamora to Montamarta is a shorter walk, around 19 km, crossing typical Castilla y León landscapes of red earth, cereal fields, and gentle hills. The terrain is mostly dirt and gravel paths with some asphalt stretches near roads, and the stage takes about 5 to 6 hours at a steady pace.

The day starts descending from Zamora city walls along quiet streets and soon joins the ZA-P-1405 road heading northeast. After about 3.5 km you leave the paved road to take the Camino de los Cascajos, a gravel path. The route then crosses the A-11 highway over a bridge. Around 6 km into the walk, you reach a roundabout with the N-630 highway, which you skirt along quieter roads such as Calle General Franco and later enter Roales de Pan town.

The Camino continues through rolling open fields with scattered trees, passing several small intersections where clear signage directs pilgrims. Around 18.5 km, a sign points off the main route to the albergue in Montamarta. The municipal albergue is about 500 meters from the town entrance with good waymarks and welcoming facilities.

Montamarta is a small village with limited services; the albergue offers a clean, quiet place for pilgrims and there is a café across from the church offering basic meals and refreshments. For more comfort, private rural homes like Vivienda Turística El Asturiano are nearby, with prices around 40 to 50 euros per night.

The stage balances a manageable distance with some mentally rewarding views and good infrastructure, making it a pleasant stopover before the longer stretches ahead. Buen Camino!

Stage 24: Montamarta to Granja de Moreruela

Stage 24 is a pleasant 22.9 km walk from Montamarta to Granja de Moreruela across typical Castilla y León countryside with red earth, farmland, and scattered oak groves. The terrain is mostly flat with few gentle slopes, featuring dirt and gravel paths along quiet rural roads.

Leaving the small village of Montamarta, the route heads north across wide fields and farmland. The way is well-marked, and pilgrims enjoy peaceful stretches with occasional birdsong and livestock sights. After roughly 10 km, the Camino crosses near the Ricobayo reservoir with scenic water views, a tranquil highlight for breaks and photos.

Granja de Moreruela is a historic village famous for its Cistercian monastery ruins dating back to 1158, a must-visit for history lovers. Accommodation includes a modern pilgrims' hostel with around ten beds, clean facilities, and year-round availability at very affordable rates (around 6 euros). Several small guesthouses and rural homes also offer rooms with local cuisine.

Pilgrims find this stage relatively easy with calmer roads, some shade, and a chance to recharge before continuing their ascent toward further mountainous stretches. Carry water and snacks as services are limited en route, and prepare for variable weather depending on the season. Buen Camino!

Stage 25: Granja de Moreruela to Tábara

Stage 25 takes you from Granja de Moreruela to Tábara, covering about 25 kilometers across the scenic landscapes of Castilla y León. The terrain features rolling hills, oak groves, pastures, and river valleys, with moderate elevation gain around 300 meters. Expect to walk for 6 to 7.5 hours at a comfortable pace, starting around 7 am after breaking your fast near the monastery ruins in Granja de Moreruela.

Begin by following the main path north, briefly traveling along the N-630 road before turning left where the route forks. Some pilgrims opt for a 4-kilometer detour to visit a historic monastery located in the Dehesa de la Guadaña area, which is worth the extra time for history buffs. The trail ascends gently over the first 3 kilometers before descending toward the Río Esla valley, offering lovely views and an excellent spot for a rest.

At around 14 kilometers, you will pass through the Valde la Rosa estate, known for its lush oak forests and peaceful surroundings—a great place for lunch or a break. Continuing on, the path leads you to Faramontanos de Tábara, a small village with café options and rural guesthouses to replenish energy supplies. The final four kilometers involve crossing a bridge and entering Tábara town.

Services along the route are limited, so carry 3 to 4 liters of water and snacks. Summer temperatures can be high, so sun protection and electrolytes are essential. The trail is marked with yellow arrows, but pay attention at several junctions, particularly near the ZA-L-2566 road and around power poles. Using offline GPS apps like Maps.me, Gronze GPX, or Wise Pilgrim will ensure smooth navigation even in areas with weak phone signal.

Safety points include careful footing on gravel paths and farm gates, occasional encounters with farm dogs (bring a stick or deterrent), and hunting seasons between October and March. Emergency services are accessible via EU 112.

Tábara is a vibrant town with a population of about 1,000 and offers several pilgrim-friendly accommodations. The Albergue Donativo is located about three-quarters of a kilometer past the center, welcoming pilgrims with over 20 beds, kitchen and shower facilities, and meals served by hospitaleros. For more comfort, the Hotel El Roble provides cozy rooms and local tapas, while several rural houses offer home-cooked meals and private rooms. It's wise to book accommodations, especially on weekends and during festival times.

This stage offers a beautiful mix of natural scenery, cultural heritage, and sufficient amenities to refresh before the next leg of the journey. Buen Camino!

CHAPTER SEVEN

Stage 26: Tábara to Santa Croya de Tera

Stage 26 from Tábara to Santa Croya de Tera spans about 22 kilometers through gently rolling terrain with minimal elevation change, making it an accessible and pleasant walk taking roughly 5 to 6 hours at a steady pace.

The route begins leaving Tábara and follows rural paths and quiet country roads with sections lined by oak trees and agricultural fields. The landscape is framed by gentle hills, with open views and intermittent shaded spots near streams and tree groves. Around 14 to 16 kilometers, you'll crest a small hill and see Santa Croya de Tera in the distance, with a downhill approach into the village.

Water and service points are limited on the trail, so pilgrims should carry sufficient water and snacks. Navigation is straightforward with clear waysigns and yellow arrows guiding through the fields and villages, although using GPS apps like Wise Pilgrim or Maps.me provides additional security as phone reception varies.

Santa Croya de Tera is a small village with several pilgrim accommodations, including the Albergue Parroquial Santa María, known for its warm hospitality and donativo pricing, offering dorm beds, kitchen facilities, and a tranquil atmosphere. Additional hostels and guesthouses provide options for varied budgets and comfort levels.

This stage offers a soothing transition with gentle terrain, ideal for resting and preparing for more challenging stages ahead. Buen Camino!

Stage 27: Santa Croya to Rionegro del Puente

Stage 27 from Santa Croya de Tera to Rionegro del Puente covers 22 km with moderate elevation gain around 250 meters across rolling hills, deciduous forests, and rural valleys in Castilla y León. The terrain mixes gravel tracks, dirt paths, and quiet roads through oak woods and farmland, taking 5.5 to 6.5 hours at steady pace; start by 7:30 am after village coffee to beat midday heat.

Hour-by-Hour Breakdown & Milestones:

- 0-5 km: Gentle climb from Santa Croya on ZA-105 briefly, then left into shaded oak forest (cool morning light, bird calls); fountain at 3 km.
- 5-12 km: Steady ascent past Calzadilla de Tera (8 km, bar/tienda for snacks); open fields with Río Tera views, watch gates.
- 12-18 km: Crest hill (peak ~800m), descend through lush woods to Olleros de Tera (16 km, café/shade oaks); dam crossing possible variant.
- 18-22 km: Flat rural lanes to Rionegro entry (pop. 200, bridge over Río Tera).

Services sparse—no mid fountains, carry 3L water/electrolytes/snacks; summer 30°C+ exposure (SPF/hat), spring wildflowers/autumn leaves ideal, winter mud/frost. Navigation: Yellow arrows clear but forks tricky (ZA roads)—Maps.me/Gronze GPX/Wise Pilgrim essential, signal weak in woods; GPX from caminodesantiagoreservas.com. Highlights: Forest shadows, valley panoramas, Sanabria tease. Pro Tip: Early start catches golden hour forests; stretch calves post-climb.

Safety & Gear: Low traffic/solo friendly (visible paths), farm dogs (stick-/DEET for ticks), loose gravel (trek poles), hunters Oct-Mar; first-aid kit (Compeed/Voltaren/ibuprofen), EU 112. Weather: Winds gusty, layerable gear.

Alternatives/Transport: Bus Santa Croya-Rionegro (~20min/8€); taxi 25€; split Olleros (16km, casa rural). Push Mombuey adds 10km beast.

Rionegro del Puente Lodging:

- Albergue de Peregrinos Virgen de la Carballeda (N-525 edge, +34 686 041 405/+34 637 124 061, mozarabesanabres@gmail.com, 10€, 20 bunks/kitchen/showers/garden).
- Casa Rural El Portal/La Fontica (25-40€ doubles/home meals).
- Hostal El Salao Restaurante (30€ rooms/tapas).

CHAPTER SEVEN

Stage 28: Rionegro to Puebla de Sanabria

Stage 28 marks an important transition as you head from Rionegro del Puente into the mountainous region toward Puebla de Sanabria. The distance is around 33 kilometers with a total ascent of about 540 meters and descent near 470 meters, making this one of the more demanding stages through rolling hills and river valleys of Zamora province. It typically takes 8 to 10 hours to complete depending on pace and conditions.

Setting out from Rionegro del Puente, the route climbs gradually and crosses diverse landscapes—oak forests, farmland, and small streams. The path sometimes follows dirt trails interrupted by roads and modern infrastructure but remains scenic, with richly varied birdlife and panoramic views. The terrain is uneven in places, so sturdy footwear and trekking poles are advisable. Navigation is generally reliable with yellow arrows, though carrying GPS apps like Wise Pilgrim or Maps.me is recommended for tricky junctions and signal gaps.

Puebla de Sanabria welcomes pilgrims with its preserved medieval charm, nestled beside a lake and backed by mountains. It offers a wide range of accommodations suitable for pilgrims, including:

- Albergue Casa Luz: well-regarded public albergue with kitchen, showers, and laundry facilities.
- Hotels such as Hotel Los Perales or Hotel Tribal, offering comfortable private rooms and local cuisine.
- Several hostels and rural guesthouses, many with WiFi and communal dining areas.

Services in town are plentiful with supermarkets, cafes, and pharmacies. Advance booking is recommended during high season or festivals to secure stays. The town provides a rich cultural experience with its castle, local museums, and traditional Galician gastronomy—a rewarding resting point before proceeding toward Galicia.

This stage blends challenge with natural beauty, historic richness, and ample amenities, perfect for a satisfying milestone on the VÍA DE LA PLATA journey. Buen Camino!

8

Chapter Eight

Galicia and Final Approach

Stage 29: Puebla de Sanabria to Lubián

Stage 29 is where you truly enter the mountains and the green embrace of Galicia. It's about 19 kilometers from the medieval town of Puebla de Sanabria, climbing steadily to the high pass of Alto de Padornelo at 1,356 meters, then descending into the small mountain village of Lubián. Expect roughly 5 to 7 hours of walking at a relaxed pace. Starting at 7 in the morning after breakfast by the castle lets you enjoy the cooler dawn air and reach the pass by midday when the views are stunning.

The first few kilometers leave Puebla on quiet country roads, crossing gentle streams and shaded trails. There is a choice between a zigzagging blue-marked trail that weaves through forests and a more direct orange-marked route close to the highway. The terrain begins to rise noticeably from around six kilometers, heading to Requejo de Sanabria village. This is the last real chance for refreshments, with a bar, café, and public fountain. Keep in mind that after rain, this area can get muddy, so check with locals or fellow pilgrims before deciding your route.

From Requejo, the climb sharpens as you push into thick pine and oak woods, eventually arriving at the Cruz del Peregrino, a high-point resting spot with benches and breathtaking views over Sanabria's lakes and valleys. Just nearby is the wind tunnel, a short but memorable stretch where gusts can surprise. From here, the path descends several kilometers to Lubián, a cozy village sitting at 1,200 meters. Lubián feels like the gateway to Galicia, small and friendly with about 250 residents.

Services along this stage are minimal—carry at least four liters of water, snacks, and sun protection. Summer fog and rain are common in this mountain zone, so pack rain gear and insect repellent for ticks. The trail is marked well with yellow arrows, but forks can be confusing; using a GPS app like Maps.me or Wise Pilgrim is recommended since cellphone reception can be spotty.

Lubián offers a few solid lodging options. The public albergue is very clean and welcoming, with dorm beds, showers, and kitchen facilities, which keep costs low. For those looking for more comfort, La Casa de Irene is a lovely rural guesthouse with garden space and BBQ, run by a friendly family, and Casa Mariana provides rooms with breakfast in the village center. Booking ahead is advisable, especially in busy months.

This stage marks a beautiful turning point—a breath of fresh mountain air, stunning natural views, and a real taste of Galician culture. Prepare well and pace yourself, as the hills here will challenge you but leave you feeling alive. Buen Camino!

Stage 30: Lubián to A Gudiña

Stage 30 from Lubián to A Gudiña is a tough one, around 24 to 30 km through Galicia's rugged mountains. You'll climb over 700 meters to the high Portela da Canda pass at about 1,300 meters, then descend into the village. Plan for 7 to 9 hours of walking at a steady pace. Leave Lubián by 6:30 or 7 am after a simple breakfast to tackle the ascent while it's cool and reach A Gudiña by late afternoon.

Picture leaving the quiet streets of Lubián and heading straight into thick pine forests on narrow dirt paths and forest tracks. The first 10 km or so rise

CHAPTER EIGHT

steadily with some steep sections where your legs will feel the burn, especially if yesterday's pass tired you out. You'll cross streams and walk through cool, shaded woods filled with birdsong and the scent of eucalyptus. Around 12 km, you hit the wind tunnel area again, similar to Padornelo, with gusts that can surprise you. From there, push up to the pass where the views open wide over rolling green hills and distant valleys, a real reward after the effort.

The descent to A Gudiña takes you along rural roads and more forest paths, passing the occasional farm or cow pasture. Services are almost nonexistent along the way, so fill your bottles in Lubián and pack plenty of snacks, nuts, and energy bars. Carry at least 4 liters of water plus electrolytes, as summer heat up here can hit 28-32°C even at elevation, and afternoon thunderstorms are common. Rain turns paths slippery, so good waterproof boots and a poncho are musts. Spring brings wildflowers, and autumn offers misty magic, but winter snow can close the pass—check forecasts.

Follow the yellow arrows closely; they are reliable but sparse in forests. Download GPX tracks from sites like caminodesantiagoreservas.com or use Maps.me and Wise Pilgrim apps, as phone signal drops in valleys. Watch for trail forks near streams and road crossings. Highlights include vultures soaring overhead, the thrill of summiting Portela da Canda with its pilgrim cross, and that first taste of Galicia's lush green carpet.

Safety first: The climbs demand fitness—use trekking poles to save your knees. Loose rocks and roots mean careful footing; ticks lurk in grass (DEET and check evenings). Farm dogs bark but rarely bite. Hunters active October to March, so bright clothing helps. Carry a full first aid kit with Compeed for blisters, ibuprofen or Voltaren for strains, antiseptic, and any personal meds. Dial 112 for emergencies; coverage is decent but spotty high up.

If it's too much, split at O Pereiro (14 km from Lubián, luxury hotel with spa) or Campobecerros. Buses run Lubián to A Gudiña (about 45 minutes, 15€), and taxis cost around 50€. Some pilgrims take the flatter road variant parallel to the N-525 to avoid steeps.

A Gudiña (pop. 1,200) sits at a road junction but feels remote and welcoming. Lodging options include:

- Albergue A Gudiña: Clean municipal spot with 20 bunks, kitchen, showers, and washing machine (10€, opens 3 pm; book ahead in summer).
- Hotel Bruma: Comfortable rooms with restaurant (40-60€, good pilgrim meals).
- Casa Rural options like Hotel Restaurante Cazador (spa vibes, 50€+, breakfast included).

Eat hearty—try local trout or caldo gallego at village bars. This stage builds your mountain legs for the finale. You've earned the views. Buen Camino!

Stage 31: A Gudiña to Laza

Stage 31 from A Gudiña to Laza winds through Galicia's rugged hills and quiet villages, covering about 31 kilometers. You will face varied terrain: forest trails with streams, rolling hills, and stretches alongside rural roads. Expect roughly 7 to 9 hours of walking at a steady, comfortable pace. Start early, around 7 am, to enjoy cooler morning air.

Leaving A Gudiña, the route climbs out of town on narrow village streets, then traverses Serra Seca, a landscape dotted with abandoned hamlets that tell stories of times past. The path undulates gently but steadily, with some steeper sections as you near Laza. Forests of oak and pine provide welcome shade, and small streams offer refreshing spots to pause.

Navigation is mostly straightforward with clear yellow arrows, but there are some intersections where extra attention is needed; using GPS apps like Wise Pilgrim or Maps.me is advised. The route passes farmland and quiet country roads, leading up to Laza, a charming town known for its stone architecture and peaceful vibe.

In Laza, pilgrims can find several accommodations including guesthouses, small hotels, and rural casas offering a range of comfort options. It's wise to book ahead, especially in the busy season. Local eateries serve hearty Galician cuisine, perfect for refueling after the day's climb.

This stage combines the feeling of deep Galicia with historical echoes of deserted villages, making it an evocative and rewarding stretch on the VÍA DE

CHAPTER EIGHT

LA PLATA. Buen Camino!

Stage 32: Laza to Xunqueira de Ambía

Stage 32 takes you from Laza to Xunqueira de Ambía over approximately 33 kilometers through Galicia's lush, rolling hills. This stage mixes forest trails, farmland, and quiet lanes, offering a sensory feast with wildflowers in spring and brilliant autumn colors. Expect 7 to 8 hours of walking at a steady pace, starting early to enjoy the cool morning air.

Leaving the town plaza, you'll soon join the OU-113 road before moving onto forest paths through oak woods and alongside small streams. The trail undulates with gentle climbs and descents, passing hamlets with hospitable locals and stopping points for water or a quick snack. The route also crosses rivers before the final approach to Xunqueira de Ambía, a town known for its 12th-century monastery and welcoming atmosphere.

The terrain is mostly firm, with some rocky sections that call for sturdy boots and trekking poles. Waymarking is clear, but using GPS apps like Wise Pilgrim or Maps.me adds confidence, especially where paths meet roads or wind through woodland. Carry enough water and snacks, as services are limited between towns.

In Xunqueira de Ambía, pilgrims find clean municipal albergues, rural guesthouses, and small hotels offering good food and rest. Booking ahead helps, especially during high season. The town's cultural treasures and peaceful setting offer a perfect pause before continuing into the vibrant city of Ourense.

This stretch brings you closer to Galicia's heart, blending natural beauty with spiritual calm. Buen Camino!

Stage 33: Xunqueira to Ourense

Stage 33 from Xunqueira de Ambía to Ourense covers about 22 kilometers and offers pilgrims a pleasant transition from rural Galicia into one of its most vibrant cities. The terrain is gently rolling with some light ups and downs as the route navigates through small villages, river valleys, and patchwork farmland. Walking time is typically 5 to 6 hours at a steady pace, starting around 7 or 8 am to enjoy cooler weather.

Leaving Xunqueira, the path heads downhill and crosses quiet lanes before intersecting with the OU-0102 road, which pilgrims follow for several kilometers. The trail includes diverse surfaces—gravel tracks, paved roads, and forest paths. Key milestones include small hamlets like A Pousa and Salgueiros that offer minimal services, so stocking up beforehand is advised.

The route crosses the scenic Río Arnoia over an ancient moss-covered stone bridge that embodies the historical depth of the region. From there, pilgrims pass through wooded paths and gentle hills before entering the urban sprawl of Ourense. The city is known for its famous thermal springs and impressive Romanesque architecture, making it a rejuvenating stop with excellent cultural and culinary offerings.

In Ourense, several pilgrim accommodations cater to all budgets:

- The municipal Albergue de Peregrinos offers kitchen and laundry facilities and is centrally located near the thermal baths.
- Private options include Albergue Augas Quentes and Grelo Hostel, both well-regarded for comfort and proximity to city attractions.
- Numerous hostels, hotels, and guesthouses also provide options for more privacy and luxury.

Pilgrims find Ourense a perfect place to rest and recharge before the final leg of the VÍA DE LA PLATA journey toward Santiago de Compostela. Booking ahead is recommended, especially during holiday seasons and festivals, due to the city's popularity.

This stage combines natural beauty, historical touchpoints, and urban vitality. It marks a gentle but meaningful step deeper into Galicia's heart. Buen Camino!

CHAPTER EIGHT

Alternative Routes: Via Sanabrés vs. joining the Camino Francés at Astorga

The Vía de la Plata offers two main final-route choices for pilgrims after reaching the northern reaches of the route: continuing along the traditional Via Sanabrés through Galicia or joining the Camino Francés at Astorga in Castilla y León.

Via Sanabrés is the historic Galician extension of the Vía de la Plata. It starts near Ourense and winds about 160 to 170 kilometers northwest through green, hilly Galicia with smaller villages, dense forests, and thermal springs. This path offers a quieter, more scenic, and more rural pilgrimage experience, rich in natural beauty and local culture. Pilgrims enjoy rustic albergues, hot springs in Ourense, and the famously lush landscapes as they approach Santiago de Compostela. The trail ends with the ascent into Santiago across the forests and hills of the Galician countryside. Via Sanabrés is perfect for those who value solitude, nature, and a connection to Galicia's cultural heritage.

In contrast, many pilgrims choose to join the Camino Francés at Astorga after completing the Via de la Plata or its extensions. Astorga is a vibrant pilgrimage town with all amenities and historical architecture, including the Gaudí-designed Episcopal Palace. The Camino Francés is the most popular Camino route, well-marked and bustling with pilgrims from all over the world. Joining here means following a highly social, infrastructure-rich path with cities, albergues, and services much more evenly spaced. The Camino Francés covers the final 200-plus kilometers through Castilla y León and Galicia, combining historical sights with larger pilgrim communities and a robust network of food and lodging options. It suits pilgrims who want a more communal experience or have less time for the longer, quieter Sanabrés.

Choosing between these alternatives depends on your priorities: Via Sanabrés for quiet nature and Galician charm, or Camino Francés for rich historical cities and crowded pilgrimage energy. Both routes converge near Santiago for the profound final arrival.

Buen Camino on whichever route you choose!

Ourense to Santiago via Sanabrés Route (overview of remaining stages)

From Ourense, the Sanabrés Route covers about 100-110 km to Santiago de Compostela, qualifying pilgrims for the Compostela certificate. This scenic, quieter extension of the Vía de la Plata winds through lush Galician countryside with forests, rivers, monasteries, and gentle hills over 6-7 stages (21-33 km each), taking 6-8 days. It's less crowded than the Francés, ideal for nature lovers seeking authentic Galicia with Romanesque churches, thermal springs, and empanadas.

Key Stages Breakdown

- **Stage 1: Ourense to San Cristovo de Cea (21 km, 3/5 difficulty):** Steady climb past Tamallancos church and Barbantiño bridge; end in bread-famous Cea.
- **Stage 2: Cea to Castro Dozón (14-17 km, 2/5):** Shaded paths to Oseira Monastery (optional detour); rural quiet.
- **Stage 3: Castro Dozón to Lalín (17 km, 2/5):** Hilltop views over farmlands and hamlets.
- **Stage 4: Lalín to Silleda (16 km, 1/5):** Easy slopes through villages and woods.
- **Stage 5: Silleda to Ponte Ulla (20 km, 2/5):** Downhill past Bandeira empanadas and hilltop castle panoramas.
- **Stage 6: Ponte Ulla to Santiago (21 km, 1/5):** Quiet rural finale via Sar district to Cathedral; emotional arrival.

Practical Essentials

- **Terrain & Weather:** Rolling paths (gravel/forest roads), 400-600m daily gain; rain frequent (poncho essential), spring/autumn best. Carry 3L water/snacks; apps like Gronze GPX/Wise Pilgrim for arrows.
- **Services:** Albergues every stage (municipal 5-12€, private 15-25€); buses

connect towns. Book peak season.
- **Highlights:** Oseira Monastery, Cea bread, thermal soaks, green valleys. Pro Tip: Split longer days; taste pulpo a feira.

This finale blends reflection and beauty—pure Galicia magic to Compostela. Buen Camino!

9

Chapter Nine

Arrival in Santiago de Compostela

The Final Approach to Santiago

The final approach to Santiago on the Sanabrés Route is a deeply moving experience. From Ponte Ulla, you head through soft green forests and quiet farms, away from city bustle. It's about 20 kilometers, taking roughly five to six hours. Most pilgrims start early, keen to reach Santiago in time for the emotional Pilgrim Mass.

You'll leave Ponte Ulla crossing a beautiful medieval bridge over the Río Ulla and walk through pine and eucalyptus groves that smell fresh and earthy. The path gently rises at first, moving past farms and occasional fellow pilgrims, but the air is peaceful and quiet, unlike the busier Camino Francés.

As you walk, keep an eye out for Pico Sacro, a sharply rising hill steeped in legend—many pilgrims pause here for a breath or some photos. The trail unfolds across golden fields dotted with traditional stone granaries called hórreos, giving a sense of timeless Galicia.

Crossing small villages, the route winds into the Sar district of Santiago. Here, modern streets give way to cobbled alleys flaming with scallop shells. Suddenly, the majestic facade of Santiago Cathedral bursts into view. Time your arrival for Pilgrim Mass when the Botafumeiro—a giant incense burner—swings through the cathedral, a moment that moves even the most stoic walker.

Bring water and snacks for the walk, as cafés are sparse until you near the city. The trail is well marked with the iconic yellow arrows and shells, but it's wise to carry a map app to stay confident, especially through the woods.

Once in Santiago, the real magic begins. Head to the Pilgrim Office to claim your Compostela certificate with your stamped credential. Then, dive into the city's delights—historic squares, lively tapas bars, and the sacred cathedral plaza, where pilgrims from all over celebrate their journey's end.

This last stretch is not just a physical walk, but a time of reflection, excitement, and joy. You've earned every step. Buen Camino!

Cathedral and Pilgrim Mass

Arriving at Santiago de Compostela Cathedral is the emotional climax of your pilgrimage. This grand Romanesque and Baroque masterpiece dominates the Praza do Obradoiro, with intricate facades and towering spires that inspire awe. The square buzzes with pilgrims every day, some limping in after weeks of walking, others radiant with joy.

Central to the cathedral experience is the Pilgrim Mass, held daily with special ceremonies on Sundays and during Holy Years. The highlight is the Botafumeiro, a giant swinging incense thurible that fills the vast nave with fragrant clouds, historically used to mask the smells of weary pilgrims. Watching the Botafumeiro in motion is a moving, almost hypnotic ritual connecting you with centuries of pilgrims before you.

The Pilgrim Mass includes blessings, singing, and moments for personal reflection. Seating is limited, so arrive early or check local listings for times. Tickets are usually free but may require reservations during peak times or special events.

Beyond the religious rites, the cathedral houses significant art, chapels, and the crypt of Saint James the Apostle. Exploring these sacred spaces offers a quieter counterpoint to the Mass's communal energy.

Visiting the Pilgrim Office nearby is an essential step. Present your stamped credential ("pilgrim passport") to receive the Compostela certificate, an official acknowledgment of completing the pilgrimage with at least 100 km walked.

The cathedral area bustles with cafés, souvenir shops, and street performers, making it a vibrant place to celebrate, rest, and connect with fellow pilgrims. This is your sacred space to savor the journey's end—rich in history, faith, and shared human spirit.

Obtaining Your Compostela

To obtain your Compostela certificate in Santiago de Compostela, there are specific steps and new rules as of 2025 that every pilgrim should know.

First, you must complete at least 100 kilometers on foot or horseback on an officially recognized Camino route. If you start outside Spain, you need to walk at least 70 kilometers within Spain. The journey can be done in stages—as long as you complete the required distance continuously and in chronological order.

One important change is that you now need to collect at least two stamps per day throughout your entire pilgrimage, not just in the last 100 kilometers. Stamps go into your pilgrim passport or credential, which you carry with you and get stamped at accommodations, churches, cafes, or tourist offices along the way. This documentation proves your pilgrimage for the Compostela.

Upon arrival in Santiago, you must go in person to the Pilgrim's Office. There, you register by scanning a QR code and providing your details. This generates a unique code which you'll use to get a ticket to collect your Compostela, the official certificate acknowledging your completed pilgrimage. A volunteer will verify your credentials and questions you briefly about your trip before issuing the Compostela.

Children may receive a special certificate if they are too young to understand the pilgrimage's spiritual nature, and they can also be included on their parents' Compostela.

No one else can collect the Compostela on your behalf. The certificate is free but requires that you personally appear at the office with your stamped credential.

Top tips for pilgrims:

- Always get your credential stamped at the start and end of each stage.
- Carry your passport securely, keep a backup copy of your stamps.
- Plan for busy times (summer, Holy Years) when lines and wait times increase.
- Enjoy the moment in the Pilgrim's Office—it's a proud and emotional milestone.

The Compostela represents more than a certificate. It marks the end of a meaningful spiritual and physical journey shared by millions over centuries. Celebrate the moment—you earned it. Buen Camino!

What to Do in Santiago: Top Sites and Experiences

Santiago de Compostela offers a rich tapestry of history, culture, and spiritual experiences that every pilgrim should savor.

1. **Explore the Cathedral:** Beyond the iconic facade, visit the crypt of Saint James, the cloisters, and the exquisite Baroque interior. Try to catch the Pilgrim Mass, where the Botafumeiro incense thurible swings above.
2. **Wander the Old Town:** Meander through cobbled streets lined with ancient stone buildings, artisan shops, lively plazas, and cafes. Stop for a café con leche and pastel de Santiago, a local almond pastry dusted with powdered sugar and the cross of Saint James.
3. **Visit the Museums:** The Museo do Pobo Galego (Museum of the Galician People) offers fascinating insights into local traditions, costumes, and crafts. The Cathedral Museum displays medieval art and relics.
4. **Relax in the Parks:** Alameda Park grants stunning panoramic views over the cathedral and city rooftops, perfect for quiet reflection or a picnic.

5. **Thermal Baths & Wellness:** Santiago has several modern spas and wellness centers that offer thermal baths, massages, and treatments ideal for weary pilgrims.
6. **Enjoy the Nightlife:** The streets around Rúa do Franco buzz with energy after dark, offering bars, tapas, and music—a great way to celebrate your journey's end.
7. **Attend Local Festivals:** If your timing is right, experience the vibrant Festa de Santiago in July with parades, fireworks, and concerts.

This blend of spiritual solace, historical beauty, and lively culture makes Santiago a perfect place to rest and celebrate the triumph of your pilgrimage. Take your time, and let the city's magic sink deep. Buen Camino!

Rest and Recovery

Rest and recovery are essential parts of your pilgrimage experience, especially after the physical and emotional demands of walking the VÍA DE LA PLATA.

Once you arrive in Santiago de Compostela or any major stop along the route, give your body time to heal and your mind a chance to reflect. Soaking in thermal baths, particularly in Ourense, can soothe tired muscles and ease aches. Many pilgrims benefit from massages, gentle stretching, and even yoga sessions designed for walkers.

Sleep is crucial—choose accommodations with comfortable beds and quiet surroundings. Use earplugs and eye masks if needed to block unfamiliar sounds and light. Hydration and nutrition play key roles in recovery, so focus on meals rich in protein, vegetables, and carbohydrates, paired with plenty of water and electrolyte drinks.

Walking slower or taking a day off mid-pilgrimage helps prevent burnout and injuries. Pay attention to blisters and minor sprains; care with Compeed patches and anti-inflammatory creams goes a long way.

Mental recovery is equally important. Journaling, talking to fellow pilgrims, or simply sitting in a quiet plaza can help process the journey's depths.

Embrace rest days as part of the pilgrimage's rhythm—they make every step after feel lighter and more purposeful. Your pilgrimage is not just about reaching Santiago, but about the transformation along the way.

Pilgrim Farewell Rituals

Pilgrim farewell rituals in Santiago de Compostela are deeply meaningful moments that mark the end of the physical journey and the beginning of a new chapter in the pilgrim's life.

Many pilgrims choose to visit the Pilgrim's Monument in the Plaza del Obradoiro to leave a token, a letter, or a note of thanks and reflection. Some write messages on ribbons or stones, symbolizing release and gratitude.

Others attend a final communal meal with fellow pilgrims, sharing stories, laughter, and the sense of camaraderie forged over hundreds of kilometers. This gathering often features traditional Galician dishes like pulpo a feira or tarta de Santiago .

A particularly moving ritual is the lighting of candles in the Cathedral or nearby chapels, sending prayers, hopes, and memories into the flickering light.

Many pilgrims also take a "last walk" around the old town streets at dusk to soak in the city's magic one final time, often reflecting in silent gratitude or with newfound friends.

These rituals help pilgrims transition from the journey mindset back to daily life, carrying the pilgrimage's peace and lessons within them forever.

III

Cultural and Historical Context

10

Chapter Ten

History of the Vía de la Plata

Pre-Roman Origins

Long before Roman legions stamped their authority, the Vía de la Plata corridor pulsed with life as one of prehistoric Iberia's most vital trade arteries. Archaeological evidence paints a vivid picture of Bronze Age networks (2500-800 BC) where Galicia's tin-rich mines fueled Mediterranean bronze production, with routes converging through today's Extremadura plains toward Phoenician ports like Huelva and Cádiz.

Key Evidence & Cultures:

- **Tartessians (Southwest Iberia):** Semi-mythical kingdom mentioned by Herodotus traded silver, ivory, and amber via western passes. Their legendary King Arganthonios (late 6th BC) allegedly hosted Phoenicians, suggesting sophisticated networks predating Carthage.
- **Celtiberians & Vettones:** Central tribes controlled highland routes, leaving oppida (hillforts) like Las Cogotas (Ávila) and castros in Galicia's Serra do Xurés. These fortified settlements guarded mineral flows.

- **Dolmens & Megaliths:** Over 300 burial chambers (e.g., Dolmen de Matillas, Salamanca) line the route, marking sacred waypoints for rituals and ancestor veneration—pilgrims today sense ancient reverence at these sites.

Trade Goods & Routes:

- **Tin from Galicia:** Essential for bronze alloy, shipped to Cornwall and Levant workshops.
- **Gold & Silver:** Lusitanian placers supplied proto-Phoenician traders.
- **Amber Road Link:** Baltic amber flowed south via Astorga, meeting Mediterranean goods.

Natural Geography: The route exploited natural saddles—Padornelo (1356m), Sanabria passes—avoiding impenetrable sierras. Seasonal herding by Vettones connected winter lowlands to summer highlands, wearing paths trodden for millennia.

Cultural Exchange: Rock art (e.g., Siega Verde, 25,000 BC) depicts hybrid motifs, suggesting Levantine influences. This pre-Roman spine facilitated Iberia's cultural melting pot, setting the stage for Roman engineering genius.

Modern pilgrims walking these ancient paths feel layered history underfoot—Bronze Age traders' ghosts whisper through cork oaks and granite milestones. Visit Numancia reconstruction or Peña Tú rock art for tangible connection.

This foundation explains why Romans chose it: millennia of human traffic had already forged the perfect northwest artery.

The Roman Road: Iter ab Emerita Asturicam

The Roman transformation of this well-used corridor into a paved imperial highway marked a new era for the route now known as the Vía de la Plata. Officially named Iter ab Emerita Asturicam , meaning "the route from Emerita [Mérida] to Asturica [Astorga]," the road was constructed under Emperor

Augustus around 25 BCE to connect the Roman provinces in Lusitania and Hispania through western Spain.

Engineers designed the road with remarkable precision. It featured meticulously laid paving stones, mile-long milestones, and regular rest stops called mansiones spaced approximately every 25 Roman miles (about 37 kilometers). These facilities provided lodging and fresh horses for Roman officials, merchants, and eventually pilgrims.

The road facilitated the efficient transport of valuable goods, especially the region's silver and gold mines, which gave the road its popular name, "Plata" (silver). It also served strategic military purposes, supporting Roman campaigns in the northwest Iberian Peninsula.

Notable Roman engineering wonders along the route include the preserved arch of Cáparra and the amphitheater and aqueduct in Mérida, a UNESCO World Heritage site. The road's enduring legacy is evident in the numerous milestones and sections of pavement that still greet pilgrims and archaeologists today.

This ancient Roman artery laid the foundations not only for trade and conquest but also for centuries of pilgrimage, cultural exchange, and regional development, making it a critical spine of Spanish and European history.

Medieval Pilgrimage Development

After Rome's fall, the Vía de la Plata endured as a shadowed lifeline through Visigothic kingdoms and Moorish al-Andalus, transforming from trade artery to Christian pilgrimage lifeline by the 9th century. The 812 rediscovery of St. James's tomb in Compostela ignited southern devotion, with Mozarabic Christians (Spanish under Muslim rule) favoring its relative safety via reconquista truces and protected valleys.

Dark Ages Revival (9th-11th Centuries)

Visigoths maintained Roman paving for armies; Moors dubbed it al-Balat ("paved road"), possibly evolving to "Plata." Almanzor's 997 raid—marching 10,000 prisoners carrying Santiago's bells to Córdoba—shocked

Christendom, spurring vows and mass pilgrimages. Bells' 1236 return via Plata symbolized reconquest triumph, drawing Andalusians north. King Alfonso II's pilgrimage (first documented) and Bishop Gelmírez's promotion cemented it.

Codex Calixtinus & Peak Popularity (12th Century)

The 1140 Codex Calixtinus (Liber Sancti Jacobi)—pilgrimage's first "guidebook" explicitly endorses Plata as visitandum est ("must-see"), detailing southern variants alongside French roads. Book V describes hospitality, miracles, and music, boosting prestige. Pilgrims surged post-1212 Las Navas de Tolosa victory, Ferdinand III securing Andalusia by 1248.

Military Orders' Protection

Knights of Santiago, Templars, and Calatrava fortified the route:

- **Puente de Zamora:** Santiago Order bridge rebuilt 1218.
- **Hospices:** Monasteries like Moreruela hosted thousands.
- **Castles:** Alba de Tormes, Sanabria guarded passes.

Pilgrimage peaked 13th-15th centuries (50,000+ annually), rivaling Francés, fueled by indulgences and royal patronage (e.g., Gran Capitán Gonzalo Fernández de Córdoba). Black Death and wars declined it by 1500s.

Legacy Along the Route

- **Mérida-Salamanca:** Mozarabic churches.
- **Zamora:** 24 Romanesque towers from pilgrim boom.
- **Sanabria:** Hermitages mark safe havens.

Revived 1980s via Xacobeos, Plata now draws 5,000 yearly adventurers tracing medieval steps amid dehesas and sierras.

CHAPTER TEN

Modern Revival and Recognition

The Vía de la Plata's modern renaissance transformed a forgotten Roman relic into Europe's premier southern pilgrimage route, blending heritage tourism, EU investment, and global Camino fever since the late 20th century.

Post-Medieval Decline (16th-19th Centuries)
  Enlightenment radial roads and railway boom eclipsed it; Napoleon's 1808-1814 Peninsular War troops rediscovered segments for logistics. Franco-era neglect left paving overgrown, milestones buried.

20th-Century Awakening (1960s-1980s)
  Father Elías Valiña Sampedro's 1980s restoration—marking arrows, clearing paths—ignited revival. His 1982 guidebook sparked local associations. Pilgrimage statistics surged from dozens to hundreds annually.

Xacobeo Holy Years & Official Status (1990s)
  1993 Xacobeo (Holy Year) exploded numbers to 5,000+ walkers; Galicia government funded signage, albergues. Council of Europe named Camino network "First European Cultural Itinerary" (1987), extending to Plata (1993). UNESCO World Heritage (1998) covered key cities (Mérida, Salamanca).

EU Integration & Infrastructure Boom (2000s-2020s)
  EU Cohesion Funds restored 80% paving/milestones; Junta de Extremadura's Plata Plan (2003) built 50+ rest areas. 2010 Xacobeo hit 272,000 total Caminos (Plata ~10%). COVID dip (2020: 50 pilgrims) rebounded to 12,000 (2024). Apps (Wise Pilgrim, Gronze) digitized GPX/stamps.

Current Recognition & Future

- **UNESCO Extensions:** Primitive Way/Plata links (2021).
- **Stats:** 5,000-15,000 yearly (2% all Caminos), 40-50 days average.
- **Awards:** Best European Heritage Trail (2022).

- **Challenges:** Overtourism mitigation, climate-resilient paths.

Today, Plata thrives as Spain's "quiet Camino"—rural solitude meets Roman ghosts, drawing adventurers tracing silver ghosts to Compostela.

Archaeological Sites Along the Route

The Vía de la Plata is a living museum of archaeological wonders, where every step uncovers layers of history from prehistoric times through Roman mastery to medieval glory. Pilgrims walk amid some of Spain's most remarkable heritage sites that tell stories of ancient civilizations, empire, and faith.

Key Archaeological Sites

- **Mérida (Augusta Emerita):** Known as the Roman capital of Lusitania, its amphitheater, theater, aqueducts, and bridge rank among Europe's best-preserved Roman ruins. The National Museum here offers extensive artifacts, while the town itself is a UNESCO World Heritage site that feels like stepping back two millennia.
- **Cáparra:** Famous for its well-preserved Roman arch gateway, this once-thriving city was a key staging post. Numerous milestones stand along the road near here, allowing pilgrims to connect tangibly with the Roman road builders.
- **Salamanca:** Beyond its university fame, this city boasts remains of Roman bridges and artifacts that mark it as a historical crossroads. Pilgrims enjoy its blend of Roman, Moorish, and Renaissance layers as part of the route experience.
- **Astorga:** The endpoint of the original Roman road, Astorga holds Roman milestones, wall fragments, and the famous Episcopal Palace by Gaudí, blending ancient and modern artistry.
- **Milestones:** Scattered along the entire route, more than 200 granite milestones survive, inscribed with imperial names and distances. Many

still stand, thrilling historians and walkers alike as direct touchpoints with the past.
- **Prehistoric Sites:** Dolmens, ancient burial mounds, and rock art in regions around Zamora and Salamanca signal the importance of this corridor long before Rome. Sites like Siega Verde offer open-air Paleolithic rock art recognized by UNESCO.
- **Monasteries & Bridges:** Medieval fortifications, including the Puente de Zamora, and monasteries such as Moreruela showcase the pilgrimage's protective infrastructure and spiritual growth through the centuries.

Walking the Vía de la Plata brings history alive with every step—from stone to spirit—offering an unmatched cultural journey through time as rich as the landscapes it crosses.

11

Chapter Eleven

Art and Architecture

Roman Engineering: Bridges, Milestones, and Roads

Roman engineers turned the Vía de la Plata into Hispania's finest highway, Iter ab Emerita Asturicam , with precision that stuns modern pilgrims. Constructed under Augustus (25 BC), it stretched 800 km from Mérida to Astorga using layered statumen (boulders), rudus (gravel), and nucleus (fine stone) over 5-6m wide beds, graded at 1:20 for drainage.

Roads: Paved Perfection

Pilgrims tread original agger (raised embankments) slabs in Extremadura (e.g., Father Blas cutaway near Aldea del Cano reveals layers). Curves minimized via surveying groma tools; winter-proof cambered crowns shed rain. Surviving stretches: Carcaboso (2km intact), Calzada de Valdunciel.

Milestones: Imperial Signposts

200+ granite miliarium cylindricum (2m tall) survive, inscribed Imp(eratori) Caes(ari) with emperors (Trajan, Hadrian), distances, curatores. Highlights:

- "Correo" milestone (Casas de Don Antonio, Cáceres): Mailbox hole.
- Carcaboso/Calzada de Valdunciel: Fountain stelai.

Bridges: Aquatic Mastery
Single-arch spans dominated; survivors:

- **Puente de Mérida:** 792m Lusitanian icon (Trajan era).
- **Alconétar (Alcántara):** 194m Tiberius bridge (Stage 13).
- **Zamora Puente de Piedra:** Medieval rebuild on Roman piers.
- **Minor gems:** Sanabria fords, Salor crossings.

Engineering Legacy: Antonine Itinerary praised it supreme; supported gold rush (Las Médulas), legions. Pilgrims touch eternity—milestones whisper 2,000 years. Visit Caparra arch (Stage 15) for immersion.

Romanesque Churches of Zamora

Zamora is famously called the city of Romanesque architecture due to its exceptional concentration of Romanesque churches and monuments, with more than 20 dating from the 11th to the 13th centuries. Pilgrims visiting the city on the Vía de la Plata are treated to a rich architectural heritage that reflects centuries of faith and frontier history.

At the heart of Zamora stands the **Cathedral of El Salvador**, a masterpiece built between the 12th and 13th centuries. It features a stunning large dome nearly 20 meters in diameter, one of the largest in Spain, and offers breathtaking views over the city. The cathedral's exterior boasts intricate sculptures and reliefs depicting religious scenes, while inside, richly decorated altars and artworks await visitors. Gothic and Baroque elements were later added to enhance its architectural depth.

Other notable Romanesque churches dot the city:

- **Iglesia de la Magdalena**, known as one of Zamora's most beautiful Romanesque churches. It stands out for its elegant design and intricate decorative elements. Gothic influences blend with its Romanesque style, creating a unique architectural gem.
- **San Pedro y San Ildefonso Church**, the largest after the cathedral, houses relics and has seen renovations that blend Romanesque origins with later styles.
- **San Claudio de Olivares**, one of the oldest in the city, retains its original austere Romanesque character with a single nave and semicircular apse.
- **Santa María la Nueva**, famous for blending Romanesque with Mudéjar elements and associated with the historic 12th-century "Trout Mutiny," features exquisite sculptural doorways.
- Smaller, charming churches like **San Cipriano**, **Santo Tomé**, and **Santa Lucía** enrich the city's cultural fabric, each with unique architectural details reflecting Romanesque traditions and later adaptations.

The city's **Plaza Mayor** and **Puente de Piedra** (Stone Bridge) provide picturesque settings surrounded by these ancient structures, inviting pilgrims to rest and absorb Zamora's medieval ambiance.

Zamora's Romanesque churches stand as timeless sentinels of spirituality and history, offering pilgrims a breathtaking window into medieval art and architecture in one of Spain's most atmospheric cities.

Gothic Cathedrals: Salamanca and Beyond

Salamanca's cathedrals are stunning highlights for pilgrims on the Vía de la Plata. The city boasts two incredible ones right next to each other, blending different styles from Romanesque to Gothic and even Baroque touches. They sit proudly in the heart of the old town, easy to visit during Stages 12 to 15.

The Old Cathedral, or Catedral Vieja, started in the 12th century with a Romanesque base that evolved into Gothic elements. Climb the Torre del Gallo, the Rooster Tower, for amazing city views. Inside, look for the Last Judgment altarpiece by Dello Delli with its 58 detailed panels, plus ancient murals and

CHAPTER ELEVEN

some of Europe's oldest pipe organs. It's cozy and full of atmosphere, perfect for quiet reflection before your next walk.

Then there's the New Cathedral, or Catedral Nueva, built from 1513 to 1733. It's Spain's last big Gothic cathedral, designed by Rodrigo Gil de Hontañón with a soaring 92-meter tower. The vast nave and chapels impress, and a neoclassical dome was added after the 1755 Lisbon earthquake. Check out the quirky astronaut carved on the exterior from a 1992 restoration joke.

Buy a joint ticket for both cathedrals, usually around 7 euros, and it works great in the morning light. Sundays are free entry. Beyond Salamanca, peek at Zamora Cathedral on Stage 22 with its huge dome, Ávila's fortress cathedral if you detour, and Ourense Cathedral on Stage 33 facing Portugal near thermal springs.

These places guided medieval pilgrims and now offer you the same sense of awe. Take your time to soak them in.

12

Chapter Twelve

Local Culture and Traditions

Festivals and Celebrations Along the Route

The Vía de la Plata comes alive with vibrant festivals that reflect each region's soul. Time your pilgrimage to join locals in joyous traditions—processions, music, feasts—that deepen your journey.

Andalusia (Stages 1-5)

- **Semana Santa (Holy Week, March/April):** Seville's world-famous processions with nazarenos, ornate pasos, and saetas fill streets nightly. Zafra's somber brotherhoods march dramatically.
- **Feria de Abril (April Fair):** Seville explodes with casetas, flamenco, sherry, and bullfights—wear traje de flamenca!
- **Romería del Rocío:** Whitsun pilgrimage to marshlands; caravans, songs, miracles.

Extremadura (Stages 6-20)

- **Carnaval de Badajoz (February):** National Tourist Interest; elaborate comparsas parade, flour fights.
- **Semana Santa Jerez de los Caballeros (Holy Week):** 8 brotherhoods, 11 processions through Badajoz's Badajoz town.
- **Festival del Queso (Cheese Festival, May):** Casar de Cáceres celebrates Torta del Casar with tastings, markets.
- **Jornadas Gastronómicas del Pitarra (September):** Zafra honors local breads.

Castilla y León (Stages 21-28)

- **Santa María de la Vega (Early September, Salamanca):** Patron saint honors with processions, concerts.
- **Semana Santa Zamora:** 24 Romanesque brotherhoods; silent, mystical.
- **San Froilán (October, Zamora):** Galicia-León fusion with music, food.

Galicia (Stages 29+)

- **Entroido Carnival Verín (Feb/March):** Galicia's wildest; cigarrón masks, fireworks.
- **Os Maios Ourense (May):** Floral sculptures, folk music.
- **Festas da Peregrina Pontevedra (August):** Virgin of Pilgrims; concerts, parties.

Pilgrim Tips: Check calendars festivals boost albergue demand—book ahead. Join processions for immersion; taste regional specialties. These celebrations remind pilgrims: camino lives beyond trails.

Traditional Cuisine by Region

The Vía de la Plata offers pilgrims a delicious journey through Spain's regional flavors. Each area's food reflects its landscape, history, and traditions. Try these local specialties at village bars and family restaurants along the way.

Andalusia (Stages 1-5)

Andalusia celebrates bold Mediterranean tastes with olive oil, fresh seafood, and cooling soups. Start your day with churros dipped in thick hot chocolate. For lunch, savor gazpacho, the chilled tomato soup perfect for hot days, or salmorejo from Córdoba, thicker with bread and egg. Fried fish like pescaíto frito shines in Seville tapas bars. Dinner means jamón ibérico, cured ham shaved thin, paired with fino sherry. Don't miss espinacas con garbanzos, spinach and chickpeas cooked with cumin and bread crumbs.

Extremadura (Stages 6-20)

Extremadura thrives on hearty inland fare from dehesa pastures and simple farms. Iberian ham rules, especially pata negra from acorn-fed pigs. Try migas, fried breadcrumbs with chorizo, garlic, and grapes, a shepherd's breakfast. Torta del Casar cheese, creamy and spoonable, pairs with local wines. Suckling pig or lamb roasted whole appears at feasts. Sopas de tomate offers tomato bread soup for rainy days. End with pitarra, homemade red wine from family vineyards.

Castilla y León (Stages 21-28)

Castilian cuisine favors robust meats and earthy flavors from the meseta. Roast lechazo, suckling lamb cooked in wood ovens, defines Zamora and Salamanca. Cocido leonés stews chickpeas, meats, and blood sausage for winter warmth. Queso de la Serena spreads like butter. Ribera del Duero reds cut rich roasts perfectly. Tapas culture thrives—try morcilla (blood sausage) or chanfaina stew. Sweet tooth? Quesadas or amarguillos almond cookies.

Galicia (Stages 29+)

Galicia's seafood kingdom meets Celtic comfort food in rainy green hills. Pulpo a feira rules—boiled octopus with paprika, olive oil, and sea salt. Empanadas, stuffed pies with tuna, cod, or meats, travel well. Caldo gallego broth warms with turnip greens, potatoes, and chorizo. Percebes (goose barnacles) thrill adventurous palates. Ribeiro or Albariño whites refresh. Finish with queimada flaming liqueur ritual banishing evil spirits, or tarta de

Santiago almond cake.

Pilgrim Tips: Ask for menú del peregrino (pilgrim menus, €10-15). Pair with regional wines. Markets offer picnic supplies. Food fuels your camino, eat local, walk happy!

Wine Regions: Ribera del Guadiana to Ribeiro

The Ribera del Guadiana wine region lies in Extremadura, spanning Cáceres and Badajoz provinces. Named after the River Guadiana, it offers diverse vineyards on flat clay soils in the Tierra de Barros sub-zone and hilly terrains in Montánchez. The climate varies from continental in the north to more Mediterranean influences in the south, creating rich conditions for both red and white wines.

Red wines dominate, especially Tempranillo, followed by Garnacha, Cabernet Sauvignon, Merlot, and Syrah. The whites shine with native grapes like Cayetana and Pardina, plus internationally known varieties like Chardonnay and Verdejo. Unique Cava sparkling wines also come from this region, mainly around Tierra de Barros.

viticulture here dates back to the 4th century BCE, with Roman mosaics showing grape harvesting. Today, modern wineries blend tradition with innovation to produce fruity young wines and quality aged blends, refreshing and vibrant with bold aromas.

For pilgrims on the Vía de la Plata, Ribera del Guadiana means a taste of Spain's rich land—pairing locally cured Iberian ham and handpicked wines for a perfect gastronomic stop. The wine route hosts tastings, vineyard tours, and festivals celebrating this heritage.

Explore the subtler contrast of Ribeiro in Galicia next for crisp whites and Atlantic breezes or journey deeper into Extremadura's heart.

Local Crafts and Products

The Vía de la Plata lets pilgrims experience Spain's rich artisan traditions that vary from region to region.

In Andalusia, famous for its vibrant ceramics from Triana, Seville, you'll find beautiful blue azulejos tiles and traditional botijos , those clay water jugs designed to keep water cool. Leather goods, especially belts and espadrilles made in Ubrique, are a local specialty. Flamenco fans can spot handcrafted castanets and exquisite shawls embroidered with stories of the dance itself. Olive oil and sherry vinegar often accompany these crafts, offering a true taste of southern Spain.

Extremadura delights with its cork crafts, creating hats, sandals, and bags from the dehesa woods where the treasured Iberian pig roams. Iron goods like horseshoes and delicate lace mantillas from Cáceres highlight the area's artisanal diversity. Food lovers will enjoy edible crafts from this region too: creamy Torta del Casar cheese, rich jamón ibérico, and the regional pitarra wines.

Castilla y León is known for its leather-bound books, an homage to the universities of Salamanca and Zamora. Zamora crafts exquisite filigree jewelry and knives, recalling medieval silversmiths. Marzipan from Astorga and robust Ribera del Duero wines bring sweetness and warmth to this high plain. Traditional wool textiles made with antique looms provide cozy layers to brave the cold nights.

Galicia's distinctive granite is carved into tiny hórreos —the traditional raised granaries—or Celtic crosses that tell stories of ancient beliefs. Burnished pottery from Buño and delicate Cambados lace showcase Galician finesse. Locally distilled queimada liqueur glasses and Albariño wine bottles celebrate the Celtic soul. Chestnuts, fresh empanada trays, and handcrafted bagpipe miniatures invite pilgrims to take home a piece of Galician magic.

When shopping, look for cooperatives (cooperativas) that preserve craft authenticity, and explore local markets (mercados) for fresh products. Keep your pack light by choosing small ceramics or foldable textiles. These treasures are not just souvenirs but memories of the camino's rich culture

CHAPTER TWELVE

and warmth.

This diverse artisan landscape enriches the pilgrimage journey with tactile traditions and heartfelt stories you can carry home.

13

Chapter Thirteen

Food and Drink Guide

Andalusian Tapas and Gazpacho

Andalusian tapas and gazpacho perfectly capture the spirit and flavors of the region. These dishes provide light, refreshing, and flavorful bites that are ideal for the warm Andalusian climate, especially during Stages 1 to 5 of the Vía de la Plata.

Tapas culture thrives as a social affair where small plates are shared among friends. Must-try tapas include pescaíto frito , small fried fish like anchovies or small hake coated in flour and fried until crispy, often served with a wedge of lemon. Jamón ibérico is world-renowned, sliced thinly from acorn-fed black Iberian pigs, often enjoyed with crusty bread or crackers called picos . Another favorite is espinacas con garbanzos , a dish of spinach and chickpeas cooked with garlic, cumin, and sometimes pine nuts or raisins, reflecting Andalusia's Moorish heritage. Don't miss albóndigas , meatballs served in tomato sauce, and the beloved patatas bravas , fried potatoes with a spicy tomato sauce.

Gazpacho is a cornerstone of Andalusian cuisine—a cold tomato-based soup made with ripe tomatoes, cucumbers, peppers, garlic, olive oil, sherry vinegar, and salt. It is blended until smooth and served chilled, often with diced vegetables, boiled egg, or ham as garnish. A thicker variation called salmorejo, originating from Córdoba, uses more bread and garlic for creaminess and is traditionally topped with boiled eggs and Ham. The porra antequerana from Málaga adds red peppers to the mix, resulting in a richer flavor.

For an authentic taste, visit tapas bars in Seville's Triana neighborhood or sample salmorejo in Córdoba's charming tabernas. Pair your meal with a glass of fino or manzanilla sherry, a refreshing low-alcohol wine that cleanses the palate between bites.

These dishes are a perfect way to enjoy Andalusian culture while replenishing your energy on the camino.

Extremaduran Specialties: Jamón Ibérico and Torta del Casar

Extremadura is famous for a few standout specialties that define the region's rich culinary heritage. Two treasures every pilgrim should try are jamón ibérico and Torta del Casar .

Jamón ibérico is the famous dry-cured ham made from black Iberian pigs, especially prized when the pigs are fed on acorns in the region's oak woodlands, or dehesa. This ham has a deep, nutty flavor and melts in your mouth, often served thinly sliced with crusty bread or as a tapa in town plazas.

Torta del Casar is a creamy, soft cheese made from sheep's milk and traditionally eaten by cutting the top and scooping out the spreadable interior with bread or vegetables. It has a robust, slightly tangy flavor and is one of the region's most celebrated cheeses.

Extremadura's food identity features rustic dishes like migas , which mixes fried breadcrumbs with garlic, chorizo, and sometimes grapes or peppers— once the humble shepherd's meal but now a favorite comfort food. Other hearty offerings include wild game stews, rich chickpea soups, and hearty vegetable dishes flavored with local paprika.

Wines like pitarra , a sweet homemade red, or sophisticated Ribera del Guadiana reds complement these dishes beautifully. Whether in taverns along the route or market stalls in Cáceres, these specialties provide a taste of Extremadura's proud and unpretentious flavors that will energize your pilgrimage steps.

Castilian Roasts and Hearty Stews

When you reach Castilla y León along the Vía de la Plata, you discover its culinary soul in rich roasts and filling stews that have fed locals through centuries of cold winters and celebrations.

One of the most celebrated dishes is lechazo asado , or roast suckling lamb. This tender lamb, milk-fed and about a month old, is seasoned simply with salt and cooked slowly in wood-fired ovens, allowing the meat to develop a crispy golden skin and melt-in-your-mouth texture. It's a family tradition served during festive occasions and special gatherings. Best enjoyed with roasted potatoes and a glass of robust Ribera del Duero red wine.

Another hearty favorite is cocido leonés , a winter stew from León packed with chickpeas, various pork cuts, sausages, vegetables, and often cecina (salted cured beef). This dish is a warming balm after a long day on the meseta, thick with smoky flavors and rich broth.

The region also boasts olla podrida , a flavorful stew combining beans, chickpeas, pork, sausages, duck, and seasonal vegetables—a filling and versatile meal with a long history tracing back to medieval cuisine.

These dishes emphasize local, high-quality ingredients prepared with care and tradition, providing pilgrims with both nourishment and a taste of Castilian heritage to savor as they continue their pilgrimage.

Galician Seafood and Pulpo

Galician seafood and pulpo a feira showcase the region's incredible ocean bounty and Celtic traditions. These dishes reward pilgrims with fresh, bold flavors perfect for Stages 29 and beyond.

Pulpo a feira , or fair-style octopus, is Galicia's signature tapa. Cooks boil fresh octopus until tender using the "scare" method, dipping it three times in boiling water to curl the tentacles just right. They slice it into rounds and serve it over boiled potatoes called cachelos, dressed with olive oil, coarse sea salt, and pimentón de la Vera paprika, either sweet or spicy. At festivals, it arrives on wooden plates, offering briny texture with smoky warmth.

Galicia's Atlantic coast supplies top seafood. Sample percebes, or goose barnacles, salty gems from rocky shores, or grilled razor clams with garlic. Sardines, hake, or monkfish fill markets. Empanada de marisco, a seafood pie, makes a great trail snack.

Pair everything with crisp Albariño or Ribeiro whites. Look for steaming pulpo pots in Ourense or Laza bars, and coastal pulperías for fresh catches. This seafood feast nourishes body and spirit through Galicia's misty paths.

Regional Wines and Beverages

Regional wines and beverages along the Vía de la Plata offer pilgrims a taste of Spain's diverse terroirs, reflecting centuries of winemaking traditions.

Starting in Andalusia, sherry wines from the Jerez and Cádiz region are a staple. These fortified wines range from dry finos with crisp nutty notes to rich, sweet cream sherries. Also popular are the crisp white wines from the Subbética mountains nearby. Traditional Iberian ham pairs wonderfully with these wines.

In Extremadura, the Ribera del Guadiana wine region produces robust reds, fresh rosés, and aromatic whites. Pitarra is a traditional homemade sweet wine typical here, enjoyed alongside local cheeses and cured meats. The region's wines are gaining recognition for their quality and ageability.

Castilla y León boasts the famous Ribera del Duero, home to some of Spain's most celebrated red wines, mostly from Tempranillo grapes. These wines are bold, with deep fruit flavors and firm tannins, excellent with the region's roasted lamb and hearty stews. The region also produces refreshing green wines from Rueda and craft cider in the northern parts.

Galicia shines with its white wines, especially Albariño from the Rías Baixas and Ribeiro from the Ribeiro region. These wines feature vibrant acidity, floral aromas, and a crisp minerality, perfectly balancing Galicia's rich seafood dishes. Lacón con grelos and Galician cider, or sidra , are also regional beverage highlights, offering fresh and tangy alternatives to wine.

Locally brewed beers and artisanal liqueurs join the mix, giving pilgrims diverse options to relax and celebrate after long walking days. Sampling these wines and drinks enriches the cultural experience, making the journey not only a physical but also a culinary adventure.

Vegetarian and Special Dietary Options

Vegetarian and special dietary options along the Vía de la Plata have improved with growing awareness, though rural areas require planning.

Spain's cuisine emphasizes fresh vegetables, legumes, and grains, making plant-based eating feasible. Common vegetarian staples include gazpacho, pisto (ratatouille-like stew), tortilla española (egg-based, vegan-adaptable), and endless salads with tomatoes, olives, and olive oil. Lentils, chickpeas, and white beans appear in hearty sopas. Bread with olive oil and tomato (pan con tomate) fuels mornings.

Vegans face more challenges in small villages where meat broths hide in soups and cheese/eggs top many dishes. Carry nuts, dried fruit, energy bars, and instant oats. Use albergue kitchens for pasta, rice, or vegetable stir-fries from local markets.

Pilgrim Strategies:

- Request sin carne (no meat) or vegetariano/vegano clearly.
- Larger towns (Seville, Mérida, Salamanca, Ourense) offer vegan spots via HappyCow app.
- Pilgrim menus (€10-15) often adapt; ask ahead.
- Markets provide picnic supplies: fruit, cheese alternatives, hummus packs.
- Galicia excels with seafood-free pulpo alternatives, seaweed salads.

Gluten-free? Corn tortillas, rice, and grilled veggies work. Notify accommo-

CHAPTER THIRTEEN

dations for celiac-safe kitchens. Apps like Wise Pilgrim list dietary-friendly albergues. Flexibility turns challenges into discoveries—local kindness prevails.

IV

Resources

14

Chapter Fourteen

Practical Directory

Tourist Offices and Information Centers

Tourist offices along the Vía de la Plata provide essential maps, stamps for your credential, local advice, and sometimes free Wi-Fi or rest areas. Most major towns have them centrally located near plazas or albergues.

Key Locations by Region
  Andalusia (Stages 1-5):

- Seville: Plaza del Triunfo 1 (Alcázar side), open 9:30am-7pm. Multilingual staff, GPX downloads.
- Zafra: Plaza Grande 1, summer 10am-2pm/5-7pm.

Extremadura (Stages 6-20):

- Mérida: Paseo de Roma, daily 9:30am-2pm/5-8pm. Roman site tickets.
- Cáceres: Plaza Mayor, 9am-2pm/5-7pm.

- Trujillo: Plaza Mayor 11, 10am-2pm/4-7pm.

Castilla y León (Stages 21-28):

- Salamanca: Plaza Mayor 32, 9am-8pm. Cathedral combo tickets.
- Zamora: Avenida de Portugal 1, 9am-2pm/4-7pm.
- Astorga: Plaza Mayor, 10am-2pm/4-6pm.

Galicia (Stages 29+):

- Ourense: Rua Progreso 5, 9am-2pm/4-7pm. Thermal bath info.
- Laza: Plaza Maior, seasonal hours.
- Santiago: Rúa do Vilar 63 (Pilgrim Office doubles), 10am-8pm.

Pro Tips: Ask for oficina de turismo or "i" signs. Smaller villages post info boards. Apps like Wise Pilgrim link locations. Staff often speak English/French; carry route name. Open hours shorten winter.

Medical Facilities Along the Route

Medical facilities are available along the Vía de la Plata, with services improving as you reach bigger towns and cities. Here is a breakdown by region:

Andalusia (Stages 1-5)

In Seville, modern hospitals like Hospital Universitario Virgen del Rocío offer comprehensive emergency care and specialist services. Smaller towns like Zafra and Mérida have health centers (centros de salud) staffed by general practitioners and nurses who can handle minor injuries typical for pilgrims.

Extremadura (Stages 6-20)

Extremadura has well-equipped hospitals in regional hubs like Cáceres (Hospital San Pedro de Alcántara) and Badajoz (Hospital Universitario de

Badajoz). Health centers across smaller stops provide basic care, wound treatment, and first aid. Pharmacy availability is good in most towns.

Castilla y León (Stages 21-28)

Salamanca features the University Hospital of Salamanca with extensive emergency and specialist departments. Zamora has a public hospital (Hospital Virgen de la Concha) offering outpatient and inpatient services. Health centers are well spread to assist pilgrims as needed.

Galicia (Stages 29+)

Ourense has the Hospital Universitario Ourense, a major medical facility with emergency care. Santiago de Compostela hosts the Hospital Clínico Universitario de Santiago, covering major medical needs including trauma and surgery.

Pilgrim Tips

- Always carry a basic first aid kit with blister plasters, antiseptic, pain relief, and any personal medication.
- Pharmacies (farmacias) are common and can provide over-the-counter remedies and prescriptions.
- In case of an emergency, dial 112 in Spain for ambulance or police assistance.
- Inform your accommodation if you have any medical conditions for quick help.

The route's medical support network is reliable, giving pilgrims peace of mind so they can focus on their journey.

Gear Shops and Services

Along the Vía de la Plata, gear shops and services are conveniently available in larger towns and cities to assist pilgrims with essential equipment, repairs, and replacements.

In Andalusia, Seville offers several outdoor and sports stores such as Decathlon and specialist hiking shops around the city center, where you can find everything from backpacks to trekking poles and comfortable footwear.

Extremadura towns like Mérida and Cáceres have local shops catering to walkers, selling basic supplies like sunscreen, hats, and gaiters. You can also find repair services for shoes and clothing.

Castilla y León's Salamanca is a hub for pilgrim gear, with multiple stores offering quality hiking boots, rainwear, electronic devices like GPS units, and energy snacks. Zamora also hosts outdoor suppliers who provide last-minute essentials and repairs.

In Galicia, Ourense and Santiago de Compostela have well-stocked shops specifically geared toward pilgrims. They carry specialized pilgrimage gear, including quick-dry clothing, walking sticks, hydration systems, and portable first aid kits.

Many albergues throughout the route also offer small shops with urgent gear and supplies, plus laundry and drying services. Several towns feature luggage transfer companies for safe and convenient transportation of your bags.

Pilgrims are advised to always carry extra socks, blister treatments, and a basic repair kit. Buying locally supports the communities and ensures you have access to region-appropriate equipment for the trail conditions.

This network of gear shops and services makes the Vía de la Plata a well-supported pilgrimage route, easing the journey's practical challenges.

CHAPTER FOURTEEN

Transport Connections

Transportation options along the Vía de la Plata are varied and offer flexibility for pilgrims depending on their needs and stage of the journey.

In Andalusia, Seville serves as a major transport hub with an international airport, high-speed train connections, and bus lines linking it to smaller towns along the route. From Seville, regular buses connect to Zafra and Mérida, facilitating flexible arrival or departure points.

Extremadura's cities like Mérida, Cáceres, and Badajoz connect pilgrims by regional trains and buses. These services run several times a day, linking pilgrimage towns and offering alternatives in case of weather delays or tired legs. Taxi services are widely available in cities and larger towns.

In Castilla y León, Salamanca has excellent train and bus connections to Madrid and nearby pilgrimage stages. Zamora offers similar regional transport links, including buses to Astorga and Puebla de Sanabria, helping pilgrims adjust daily distances or reach accommodations.

Galicia's Ourense and Santiago de Compostela cater to pilgrims with train stations on the high-speed AVE line and frequent buses. Santiago's airport offers domestic and some European flights, ideal for starting or ending the pilgrimage.

For inter-city travel, national rail and bus companies like Renfe and ALSA provide scheduling and ticketing for convenient planning along the route.

Pilgrims often use taxis or private transfers for short distances, especially when navigating stage variations or early morning starts.

Combining walking with planned transport options helps manage the journey's pace, ensuring both challenge and comfort.

Luggage Transfer Services

Luggage transfer services on the Vía de la Plata are less comprehensive than on busier routes like the Camino Francés, but reliable options exist, especially from Extremadura onward.

Available Services:

- **Pilbeo**: Covers Camino Sanabrés (Ourense to Santiago). €28 per bag/stage, max 20kg. Pickup 8-9am, delivery by 2:30pm. Book via app/website: pilbeo.com. Real-time tracking.
- **Correos (Spanish Post)**: Reliable from Ourense to Santiago. Paq Peregrino service; book at elcaminoconcorreos.com. Affordable, widespread offices.
- **Servicios Camino Sanabrés**: Private service from Granja de Moreruela. Contact: servicioscaminosanabres@gmail.com or +34 674 56 98 70. Custom pricing.

Early Route (Seville to Granja de Moreruela):

No dedicated door-to-door services. Arrange taxis (€1.50/km) or local vans through albergues/hostales. Pilgrims negotiate directly—Spanish helpful.

General Tips:

- Max 1 bag/person, 15-20kg. Use ID tags/labels.
- Book 1-2 weeks ahead (peak season).
- Confirm pickup times (often 8am); late arrivals risk delays.
- Smaller villages: Drop at bar/albergue for forwarding.

Alternatives: Walk light (10kg pack), ship extras to Santiago via Correos, or use hybrid taxi transfers. Services improve post-Ourense.

Useful Apps

Useful apps for pilgrims walking the Vía de la Plata help with navigation, accommodation, weather, and community connection.

- **Wise Pilgrim**: Offers detailed maps, GPX files, accommodation guides, weather updates, and elevation info. Great for offline use and planning

daily stages.
- **Maps.me**: Essential offline GPS navigation with route tracking, nearby services, and user contributions for trail conditions and accommodations.
- **Google Maps**: Useful for urban navigation, transport planning, and real-time traffic or public transport updates.
- **PILBEo**: A dedicated app for booking and tracking luggage transfer services on the Camino Sanabrés segment.
- **El Tiempo**: Spain's reliable weather forecasting app to plan your walking days with safety in mind.
- **Facebook Groups & Forums**: Communities like "Vía de la Plata Pilgrims" provide real-time advice, meetups, and support.
- **Airbnb**: Helpful for locating and reserving lodgings not listed on pilgrim-specific platforms.

Having these apps downloaded and ready before starting your pilgrimage greatly enhances convenience and safety while keeping you connected with fellow walkers and local resources.

15

Chapter Fifteen

Spanish Language Guide

Essential Phrases for Pilgrims

Here is a selection of essential Spanish phrases useful for pilgrims on the Vía de la Plata. These will help you navigate accommodations, meals, medical needs, and general conversation:

Greetings and Basics

- Hola – Hello
- Buenos días – Good morning
- Buenas tardes – Good afternoon
- Adiós – Goodbye
- Por favor – Please
- Gracias – Thank you
- Lo siento – Sorry
- ¿Habla inglés? – Do you speak English?

Accommodation and Services

CHAPTER FIFTEEN

- ¿Dónde está el albergue? – Where is the albergue?
- ¿Tiene cama libre? – Do you have a free bed?
- Quisiera reservar – I would like to reserve
- ¿Cuánto cuesta? – How much does it cost?
- La cuenta, por favor – The bill, please

Food and Dietary

- Menú del peregrino – Pilgrim menu
- Agua – Water
- Vino – Wine
- Sin carne – Without meat
- Vegetariano/a – Vegetarian

Medical and Emergencies

- ¡Ayuda! – Help!
- Farmacia – Pharmacy
- Hospital – Hospital
- Me duele aquí – It hurts here
- Ampolla – Blister

Directions and Numbers

- Izquierda – Left
- Derecha – Right
- Recto – Straight
- Estoy perdido/a – I am lost
- Uno, dos, tres, cuatro, cinco – One, two, three, four, five

Cultural Etiquette Tips

- Greet with Buenos días or Buenas tardes.

- Use Por favor and Gracias frequently.
- Two kisses on the cheek are a common greeting.
- Dress modestly, especially in churches.
- Say Buen provecho to others before eating—it means "enjoy your meal."

Learning and using these phrases will create smoother, friendlier experiences, especially in rural areas along the route. Locals appreciate your efforts, and it enriches your pilgrimage journey. Buen Camino!

Menu Vocabulary

Knowing key Spanish food terms helps pilgrims order confidently along the Vía de la Plata, especially when requesting the affordable menú del peregrino (pilgrim menu).

Beverages

- Agua – Water
- Cerveza – Beer
- Vino tinto – Red wine
- Vino blanco – White wine
- [Zumo} – Juice
- translate:Agua con gas – Sparkling water

Basics and Starters

- Pan – Bread
- Ensalada – Salad
- Sopa – Soup
- Caldo – Broth
- Ensaladilla rusa – Russian salad
- Gazpacho – Cold tomato soup

Main Dishes

- Pollo – Chicken
- Carne – Meat
- Pescado – Fish
- Jamón – Ham
- Chorizo – Sausage
- Tortilla – Omelette/Spanish potato omelette
- Cocido – Stew
- Migas – Fried breadcrumbs

Sides and Vegetables

- Patatas fritas – French fries
- Verduras – Vegetables
- Judías verdes – Green beans
- Pimientos – Peppers

Desserts

- Flan – Custard
- Tarta de Santiago – Almond cake
- Fruta – Fruit
- Helado – Ice cream

Useful Phrases

- Menú del peregrino – Pilgrim menu
- ¿Qué recomienda? – What do you recommend?
- Sin carne – No meat
- Vegetariano/a – Vegetarian
- La cuenta, por favor – The bill, please

Print this list or save it on your phone. Locals appreciate the effort, and it unlocks authentic regional flavors. Buen provecho!

Medical and Emergency Terms

Here are essential medical and emergency terms in Spanish to help pilgrims along the Vía de la Plata:

- ¡Ayuda! – Help
- Emergencia – Emergency
- Médico – Doctor
- Enfermero/a – Nurse
- Hospital – Hospital
- Farmacia – Pharmacy
- Ambulancia – Ambulance
- Me duele aquí – It hurts here
- Ampolla – Blister
- Me siento mal – I feel sick
- Tengo alergia a … – I'm allergic to …
- ¿Dónde está el hospital más cercano? – Where is the nearest hospital?
- Llame una ambulancia – Call an ambulance
- No puedo respirar – I can't breathe
- Estoy mareado/a – I feel dizzy
- Perdí el conocimiento – I lost consciousness
- Necesito un médico – I need a doctor

For any emergency situations, dial 112 to reach emergency services in Spain. Being familiar with these terms can make a crucial difference if you need medical assistance on the route. Keep a small phrase card or notes with you for quick reference as you walk.

CHAPTER FIFTEEN

Numbers, Days, and Directions

Knowing basic numbers, days of the week, and directions in Spanish helps pilgrims navigate the Vía de la Plata more confidently.

Numbers

- Uno – One
- Dos – Two
- Tres – Three
- Cuatro – Four
- Cinco – Five
- Diez – Ten
- Veinte – Twenty

Days of the Week

- Lunes – Monday
- Martes – Tuesday
- Miércoles – Wednesday
- Jueves – Thursday
- Viernes – Friday
- Sábado – Saturday
- Domingo – Sunday

Directions

- Izquierda – Left
- Derecha – Right
- Recto – Straight ahead
- ¿Dónde? – Where?
- Estoy perdido/a – I am lost

This set covers what you need to ask for directions, understand schedules, and communicate basic numeric information on your journey. Remember that in Spanish, days of the week are not capitalized unless starting a sentence.

Using these words will help you get around villages, find the albergue, and engage with locals for a safer, richer pilgrimage experience.

Cultural Etiquette

Respecting Spanish customs along the Vía de la Plata enhances your pilgrimage and builds warm connections with locals.

Greetings and Politeness

Always greet with Buenos días (good morning, before noon) or Buenas tardes (good afternoon). Use Por favor (please) and Gracias (thank you) generously. Friends and acquaintances exchange two kisses on the cheeks, starting with the right.

Dining Customs

Say Buen provecho (enjoy your meal) before eating. Wait for "¡Salud!" (cheers) before sipping drinks. Siesta means shops close 2-5pm—respect quiet hours. Tipping 5-10% in restaurants shows appreciation.

Religious Sites

Dress modestly (cover shoulders/knees) in churches. Silence during services. Remove hats inside. Flash photography often prohibited.

Camino-Specific Etiquette

- Greet fellow pilgrims with Buen Camino .
- Yield to cyclists; announce passing.
- No littering—carry trash to bins.
- Albergues: Earplugs essential, short showers, no snoring complaints.
- Buy something before using bar toilets.

CHAPTER FIFTEEN

General Tips

Speak slowly, smile—effort appreciated. Avoid criticizing local ways. Siesta respected; early dinners (8-10pm) common. Personal space smaller than northern norms.

These practices create harmony, turning strangers into friends.

Nightlife and Entertainment

The Vía de la Plata offers pilgrims relaxed evening entertainment in historic plazas and cozy bars rather than wild clubbing, perfect for unwinding after long walking days.

Andalusia (Stages 1-5)

Seville pulses with flamenco tablaos like El Arenal and La Carbonería, where passionate duende fills intimate venues. Triana bars serve tapas with live guitar. Zafra's Plaza Grande hosts summer concerts under castle lights.

Extremadura (Stages 6-20)

Mérida's Roman theater hosts summer opera festivals. Cáceres old town bars pour pitarra wine amid medieval alleys. Trujillo's Plaza Mayor features folk music evenings and artisan markets.

Castilla y León (Stages 21-28)

Salamanca's Plaza Mayor buzzes with student bars, live jazz, and summer verbenas dances. Zamora's Romanesque churches host classical concerts. Astorga's Gaudí palace area offers cozy pub crawls.

Galicia (Stages 29+)

Ourense thermal bars blend hot springs with Galician folk. Santiago's Rua do Franco lines with pilgrim pubs, gaita (bagpipe) sessions, and queimada rituals. Laza fiestas feature Celtic music.

Pilgrim Tips: Evenings start late (10pm+). Dress casual but neat. Join locals for authenticity—expect ¡Salud! toasts. Albergue common rooms foster storytelling. Festivals amplify fun; check calendars.

BUDGET PLANNER

Category	Item/Details	Estimated Cost (€)	Actual Cost (€)	Notes
Travel & Transport				
a. Flights	(To/from Spain)			
b. Trains/Buses	Regional & local routes			
c. Taxis/Transfers	Airport, station, towns			
d. Other transportation	Bike rentals, shuttles			
Accommodation	Hostels, albergues, hotels			Include nightly rates
Food & Drink	Breakfast, lunch, dinner			Daily estimate

BUDGET PLANNER

Category	Item/Details	Estimated Cost (€)	Actual Cost (€)	Notes
Equipment & Supplies	Gear, clothes, toiletries			One-time and ongoing costs
Medical & Emergency	Medications, first aid			Emergency fund
Activities & Extras	Sightseeing, tours			Museums, special outings
Souvenirs & Gifts	Local crafts, souvenirs			Budget for gifts
Contingency Fund	Unexpected expenses			Usually 10-15% of total
-------------------	-------------------	-------------------	-------------------	-------------------
Total Budget				

TRAVEL JOURNAL

TRAVEL JOURNAL

My VÍA DE LA PLATA Hiking Journal

Every step you take leads you closer to your final destination.

✳ Day ___ :
_____

Camino Português Travel Journal

📍 Route & Distance

Starting point: _____

Destination: _____

Distance walked today: _____ km

Time started: _____ am / Time arrived: _____ pm

Weather today: ☀ 🌧 ❄ 🌬 ⛅

Walking Experience

What stood out to you on the path today?
→ _____

→ _____

Describe one challenge you faced (physical or emotional).
→ _____

What gave you strength or motivation to keep going?
→ _____

Spiritual or Emotional Reflection

How did you feel when you started this morning?
→ _____

Did you have any moments of silence, prayer, or insight?
→ _____

What did you learn about yourself today?
→ _____

People & Encounters

Who did you meet or walk with today?
→ _____

What story, advice, or kindness touched you most?
→ _____

Food & Culture

What did you eat or drink that you'll remember?
→ _____

Describe something beautiful or unique you saw today — a view, a church, a smell, a sound.
→ _____

End-of-Day Thoughts

Accommodation: _____

How comfortable was it? ★ ★ ★ ★ ★

How do you feel right now (physically & emotionally)?
→ _____

Daily Gratitude

Today, I am grateful for…"
→ _____

→ _____

Quote of the Day (optional)

Write an inspiring line you heard or thought of today:
→ _____

_____

Tomorrow's Intention

What do you hope for or focus on tomorrow?
→ _____

_____

TRAVEL JOURNAL

✳ **Day __ :**
_____

Camino Portugués Travel Journal

📍 **Route & Distance**

Starting point: _____

Destination: _____

Distance walked today: _____ km

Time started: _____ am / Time arrived: _____ pm

Weather today: ☀ 🌧 ❄ 🌫 ⛈

Walking Experience

What stood out to you on the path today?
→ _____

→ _____

Describe one challenge you faced (physical or emotional).
→ _____

What gave you strength or motivation to keep going?
→ _____

Spiritual or Emotional Reflection

How did you feel when you started this morning?
→ _____

Did you have any moments of silence, prayer, or insight?
→ _____

What did you learn about yourself today?
→ _____

People & Encounters

Who did you meet or walk with today?
→ _____

What story, advice, or kindness touched you most?
→ _____

Food & Culture

What did you eat or drink that you'll remember?
→ _____

Describe something beautiful or unique you saw today — a view, a church, a smell, a sound.
→ _____

_____

End-of-Day Thoughts

Accommodation: _____

How comfortable was it? ★ ★ ★ ★ ★

How do you feel right now (physically & emotionally)?
→ _____

Daily Gratitude

Today, I am grateful for…"
→ _____

→ _____

Quote of the Day (optional)

Write an inspiring line you heard or thought of today:
→ _____

_____

Tomorrow's Intention

What do you hope for or focus on tomorrow?
→ _____

_____

VÍA DE LA PLATA CAMINO TRAVEL GUIDE

✳ **Day __ :**
_____

Camino Portugués Travel Journal

📍 **Route & Distance**

Starting point: _____

Destination: _____

Distance walked today: _____ km

Time started: _____ am / **Time arrived:** _____ pm

Weather today: ☀ 🌧 ❄ 🌫 ⛈

Walking Experience

What stood out to you on the path today?
→ _____

→ _____

Describe one challenge you faced (physical or emotional).
→ _____

What gave you strength or motivation to keep going?
→ _____

TRAVEL JOURNAL

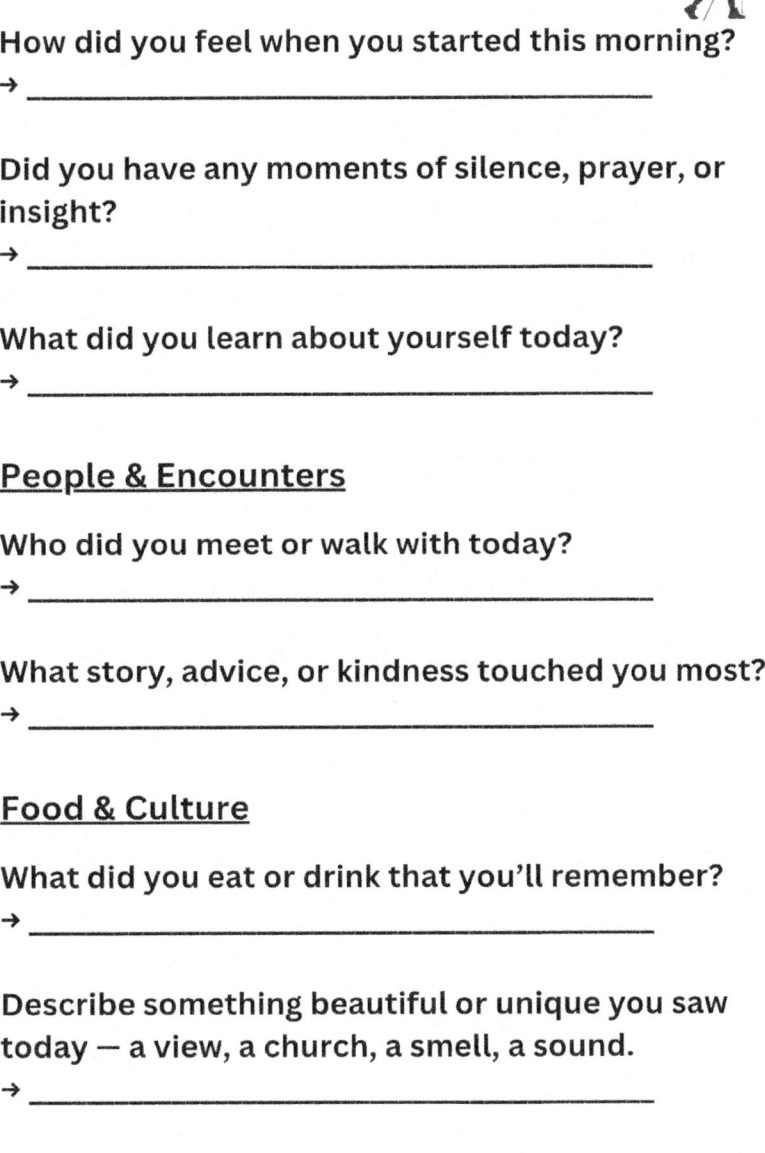

Spiritual or Emotional Reflection

How did you feel when you started this morning?
→ _____

Did you have any moments of silence, prayer, or insight?
→ _____

What did you learn about yourself today?
→ _____

People & Encounters

Who did you meet or walk with today?
→ _____

What story, advice, or kindness touched you most?
→ _____

Food & Culture

What did you eat or drink that you'll remember?
→ _____

Describe something beautiful or unique you saw today — a view, a church, a smell, a sound.
→ _____

_____

End-of-Day Thoughts

Accommodation: _____

How comfortable was it? ☆ ☆ ☆ ☆ ☆

How do you feel right now (physically & emotionally)?
→ _____

Daily Gratitude

Today, I am grateful for…"
→ _____

→ _____

Quote of the Day (optional)

Write an inspiring line you heard or thought of today:
→ _____

_____

Tomorrow's Intention

What do you hope for or focus on tomorrow?
→ _____

_____

Printed in Dunstable, United Kingdom